origami

& other paper creations

First published in Great Britain in 2013 by Search Press Limited,
Wellwood, North Farm Road, Tunbridge Wells, Kent TN2 3DR

Original edition © 2012
World rights reserved by Éditions Marie Claire
Original French title: *Origami & créations en papier*

Designs: Ghylenn Descamps
Photography: Jean-Baptiste Pellerin
Styling: Dominique Turbé
Graphic design and layout: Either Studio

ISBN: 978-1-8448-993-0

All rights reserved. No part of this book, text, photographs or illustrations may be reproduced or transmitted in any form or by any means by print, photoprint, microfilm, microfiche, photocopier, internet or in any way known or as yet unknown, or stored in a retrieval system, without written permission obtained beforehand from Search Press Limited.

Printed in Malaysia

ACKNOWLEDGMENTS AND PHOTO CREDITS

The author would like to give particular thanks to the following:
Fifi Mandirac for her beautiful papers, which are so fresh, colourful and cheerful.
Adeline Klam for her marvellous Japanese papers, which are so inspiring.
La Droguerie for all the little treasures that we found in its Rennes shop enabling us to make the jewellery and other lucky charms in this book.

All photographs by Jean-Baptiste Pellerin except page 7 from Fotolia

Also with gratitude to:
Lalé (www.lale.fr): kit bag p. 26
Ladurée (www.laduree.fr): box p. 51
Fleux (www.fleux.com): porcelain key p. 77, bowl p. 97, porcelain rabbits p. 114
Petit pan (www.petitpan.com): paper p. 114
Miniseri (www.miniseri.com): satchel p. 144

origami

& other paper creations

ghylenn descamps

Search Press

contents

the origins of origami	6
about this book	6
choice of paper	8
basic advice and tools	10
jewellery and lucky charms	12
office stationery	34
decorations for the home	56
at the table	82
celebrations	98
for children	122

The word origami comes from the Japanese 'Ori', to fold, and 'Kami', paper. It literally means: folding of paper.

the origins of origami

The art of origami originated in the Far East. The Chinese invented paper in the second century A.D. and, consequently, the Japanese learned how to produce it from travelling monks some 400 years later. After some time the Japanese abandoned the Chinese production techniques and each region of Japan developed its own style.

Paper was originally a precious commodity reserved for the elite, but gradually its use extended to daily life in the form of *shoji* (sliding, paper screens), *chochin* (lanterns) and *sensu* (folding fans). The Edo Era (1603–1867) witnessed an increase in production of paper and its use spread throughout the population.

While the precise origins of origami are difficult to trace, the oldest known work dedicated to origami is recognised as 'Hiden Senbazuru Orikata' (1797), which demonstrates how to make the 'garland of 1000 cranes', the secret of folding 1000 cranes each linked to one another.

It was during the World Exhibition in Vienna in 1873 that the West discovered the Japanese craft of origami, which, until then, was unknown in Europe.

The delicate art of origami soon seduced the world and became a resounding success due to the importation of magnificent Japanese papers and the technique's combination of simplicity and complexity.

about this book

Origami is suitable for all ages, and easily achievable with a little experience and patience.

Some of the items in this book are very simple to make and others are a little more complex. The designs focus not only on traditional origami models, but also on inventive and decorative ways to use the gorgeous range of papers that is now available. All the projects are designed to be decorative as well as useful in daily life, and they make great presents that will delight your loved ones. So enjoy the making process and have fun with your creations!

choice of paper

In Japan, there is an impressive variety of beautifully patterned origami paper. However, when starting out, it is best to use copier paper (maximum 80gsm/54lbs) or brown craft paper. Craft paper has the advantage of being coloured on both sides. You will need to cut the paper into squares before starting your folding.

These days, pre-cut, plain or two-tone blocks cut into squares of different sizes are available for origami lovers. Some are printed with patterns and come in different thicknesses or weights per square metre. Some are coloured on both sides.

Japanese 'washi' paper is fine, flexible and strong, available in plain or patterned sheets made from natural fibres and is ideal for origami. The patterns are inspired by those of traditional kimonos and it is difficult to choose a favourite, as they are all so beautiful! This paper comes in different sizes as well.

There are other papers that are perfect for origami too, even if they are not Japanese:
- fine, flexible gift wrap, which comes in a wide range of patterns and colours (ensure that you buy good quality paper, as some patterns can wear off)
- white or coloured lightweight drawing paper: Ingres or Velin
- fibrous papers such as banana or mulberry, which come in a light weight and in beautiful colours
- chalk or crystal paper
- silk paper or even organza fabric
- newspaper and magazines.

You can use any paper as long as it folds easily without spoiling or tearing and is easy to work with, without losing its shape. That is why fine paper is more suitable; thicker paper is sturdier and is better for papercutting.

basic advice and tools

where can you find paper?

Fortunately, there is no need to go to Japan to find Japanese paper. You can find it in:
- art shops
- stationers or specialist departments
- Japanese shops
- online, on websites that offer a wide range of imported paper.

basic advice

- Work on a flat surface that is clean and cleared.
- Take time to really understand the folding design and the steps.
- Check that the square is perfect and check the dimensions of the chosen model. If necessary, place a set square on the paper. Cut with a craft knife and a ruler on a cutting mat. If the sheet is not of the required size, draw a corner with the set square, transfer the desired measurement and cut the paper using the craft knife and the ruler.
- Practise folding several times using copier paper or craft paper in larger sizes to really understand the folding. Then reduce the size, in several stages if necessary. Make sure you feel ready before folding with your chosen paper.
- Have the recommended tools and materials within reach at the start.
- Start with very simple folding. Traditionally, making the crane (see page 15) is an ideal start, as it helps you to learn most of the basic folds, however you can choose to start with easier folding.

basic tools

Origami is a simple technique that requires few tools: the only indispensable tool is a paper folder! Paper folders are made from either bone or plastic and enable the folds and points to be scored clearly without damaging the paper.

The other tools used in this book are:
- a pencil for marking out
- a ruler to measure the paper and guide the craft knife
- a craft knife for cutting the paper
- a cutting mat for cutting the paper
- a set square to check that the paper is square or to use as an outline
- a pair of scissors to make little cuts
- a tube of adhesive for small areas
- a pot of white vinyl adhesive to stick cardboard
- a paintbrush to paint on the adhesive.

You may also sometimes need:
- a compass
- a black felt-tip pen
- a tube of black paint
- a fine paintbrush.

jewellery and lucky charms

jewellery and lucky charms

crane earrings

difficulty

MATERIALS FOR ONE PAIR OF EARRINGS
2 squares of origami paper 5 x 5cm (2 x 2in) ♦ 1 pair of earring findings ♦ 2 earring findings with loops ♦ 1 fine chain 20cm (7¾in) long ♦ 2 end fasteners for fine chains ♦ matching rings ♦ twisted wire ♦ crimp beads ♦ matching beads ♦ lacquer

EQUIPMENT
1 pair of wire-cutting pliers ♦ 1 sewing needle ♦ 1 paper folder ♦ 1 paintbrush

folding

1. Score the centre lines and the diagonals. Fold to the rear along the diagonal.
2. Score the fold along the dotted line and unfold.
3. Lift the top point over towards you.

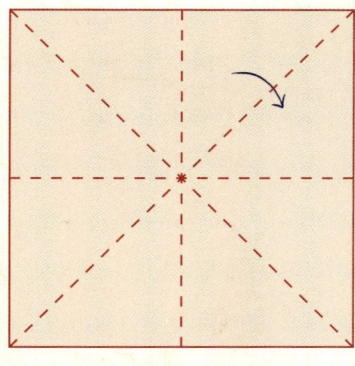
1

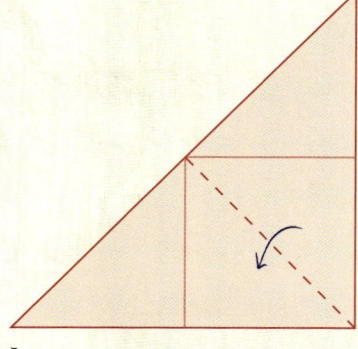
2

3

crane earrings (cont.)

4. Open with the help of the scored creases.
5. Flatten and score the folds. Turn the folding over.
6. Repeat steps 3 to 5 with the point formed. Flatten out the folds.
7-8. Turn the folding by a quarter turn.
9. Fold the top sheets along the dotted lines.
10. Turn the folding over and fold along the dotted lines.
11. Fold over the point.
12. Unfold the point and the sides of the triangle.
13. Take the bottom point and unfold it towards the top with the help of the creases.
14. Stretch out to the top.
15. Score the folds.

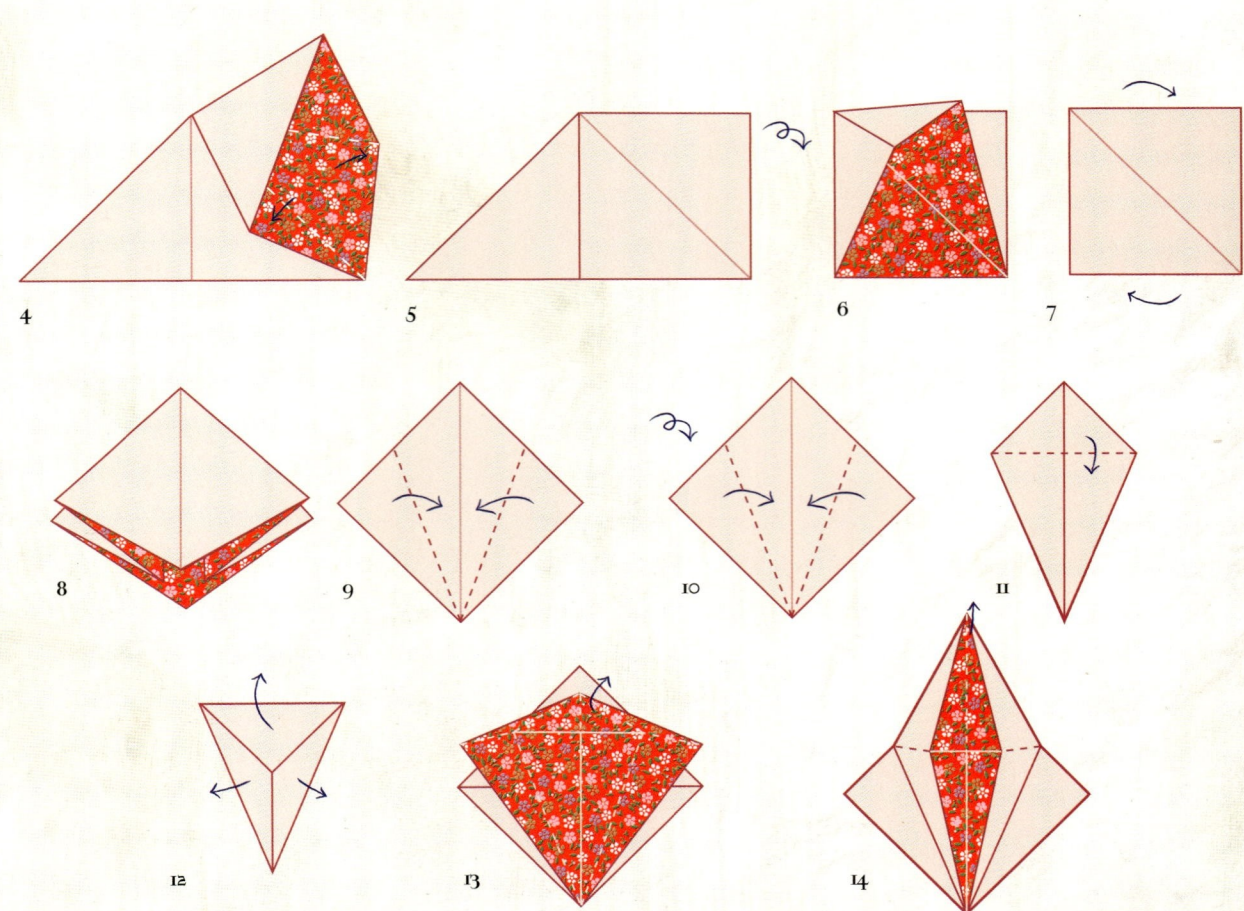

jewellery and lucky charms

16. Fold the top sheet along the dotted lines.
17. Score the folds. Turn the folding over and repeat steps 15 and 16.
18. Fold along the dotted lines.
19. Separate the bottom points and invert the folds by bringing the points up towards the top. Score the folds.
20. Score the fold for the head by inverting it to make the head of the crane. Gently separate the wings away from the body. Lacquer and leave to dry.

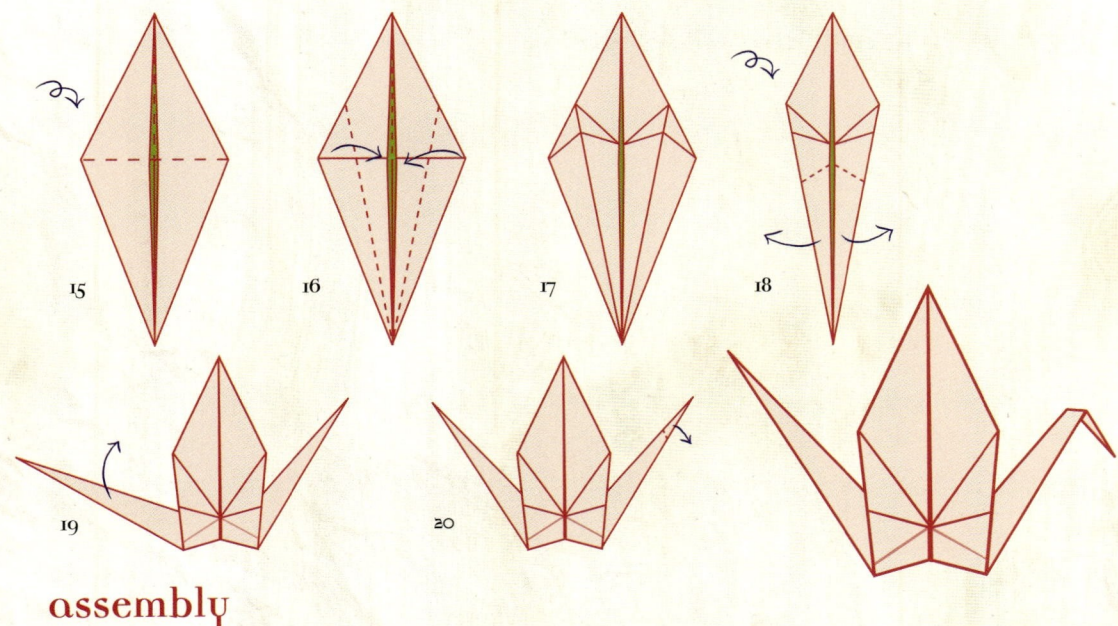

assembly

Gently pierce one crane through the centre using a sewing needle.
 Cut the fine chain into four using a pair of pliers. Attach two pieces to one end fastener. Pull one of the matching rings apart and slide on the end fastener with the two chains attached. Attach an earring finding with loop to this ring and then close it up again. Insert the end of the earring finding inside the body of a crane. Using a pair of pliers, make a loop with the end of the earring finding, which is inside the crane. Thread the twisted wire into the loop you have just made. Now make a new loop with the twisted wire and close it up with a crimp bead. Cut off one of the excess ends of the wire leaving one strand to slide on a bead and another crimp bead. Loop the end of this wire into another matching ring then back into the crimp bead, forming a closed link around the matching ring. Cut off the excess wire. Slide the matching ring on to an earring finding.
 Assemble the second earring in the same way.

jewellery and lucky charms

necklace

difficulty

MATERIALS
2 sheets of patterned origami paper 25 x 25cm (9¾ x 9¾in) ♦ 1m (1yd) of plum organza ribbon 5mm (¼in) wide ♦ 2 x 1m (1yd 3in) of grey coated cotton thread ♦ DMC no. 321 red stranded cotton thread ♦ mauve beads ♦ red sewing thread ♦ 1 fastener ♦ lacquer

EQUIPMENT
1 pair of scissors ♦ 1 compass ♦ 1 pair of pliers ♦ 1 tube of adhesive ♦ 1 pencil ♦ 1 sewing machine ♦ 1 paintbrush

assembly

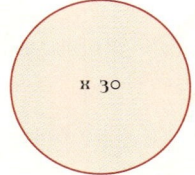

flat bead :
2cm (¾in) diameter

Draw 30 circles of 2cm (¾in) diameter on to the reverse of some origami paper and cut them out with a pair of scissors. Put two of the circles away on one side and glue the remaining 28 together in pairs to form 14 discs.

Draw six discs of 3cm (1¼in) diameter and cut them out. Glue them together in pairs, forming three discs. Lacquer all the discs with the paintbrush and leave to dry.

Machine stitch the discs together using the red sewing thread and position the three larger discs in the centre of the necklace leaving a space of around 2cm (¾in) between each disc. Slide a mauve bead on to some grey coated cotton thread and secure with a knot at either side. Place a bead approximately every 7cm (2¾in).

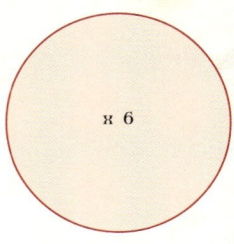

large flat bead :
3cm (1¼in) diameter

Make a hole on the edge of the centre disc. Fold in half several 20cm (7¾in) long strands of red stranded cotton thread. Push the looped thread into the hole in the disc and then pass the ends of the thread through the loop, gently pulling tight to secure. Next, glue the two remaining circles together allowing the red stranded thread to pass between them. Hold it firmly in place while the adhesive dries.

Assemble the components of the necklace: the string of paper discs, the ribbon and the grey cotton thread, and attach a fastener to them at the end of each, stringing them all together.

NB: To achieve a graduated look to the necklace, reduce the length of both the ribbon and the grey beaded thread by 1cm (½in).

hair grips with stars

jewellery and lucky charms

beaded necklace

MATERIALS
1 square of red origami paper 6.5 x 6.5cm (2½ x 2½in) ♦ 1 square of yellow origami paper 4 x 4cm (1½ x 1½in) ♦ 80cm (31½in) of red coated cotton thread ♦ 80cm (31½in) of fuchsia pink coated cotton thread ♦ crimp beads ♦ red beads ♦ 1 headpin ♦ 1 headpin with loop ♦ 2 small bead caps ♦ 2 large bead caps ♦ 1 ring ♦ 2 cord ends ♦ 1 fastener

EQUIPMENT
1 pair of pliers ♦ 1 needle

folding

1. For both the red and yellow papers: first fold along the centre lines then the diagonals as indicated by the dotted lines. Unfold.
2. Fold the square in half with a horizontal fold.
3. Open the right corner as shown in the diagram. Flatten down the crease line to create a triangular fold. Press firmly into place.
4. Turn the left point of this triangle back towards the right forming a crease along the dotted line shown.
5-6. Now take the top left corner and open it to form a triangle fold, as in step 3. As in step 4, turn the corner back so your design resembles the image in Fig. 6.
7. Fold along the dotted lines so the corners of the first sheet meet the top.
8. Flatten and flip the whole design over.
9. On this side, repeat step 7 to create a small square shape.
10. Fold over the right and left points of the first sheet along the dotted lines and make a crease.
11-12. Fold over the two top points of the first sheet along the dotted lines.
13-14. Following the diagrams, fold the edges neatly into the sheets of the centre triangles, by allowing the fold to create a three-fold shape that should concertina into its centre triangle.
15. Turn the folding over and repeat steps 10 to 14.
16. Fold along the dotted lines and unfold.
17. Unfold and gently separate the tips of the square. Blow into the little opening until the cube takes shape.

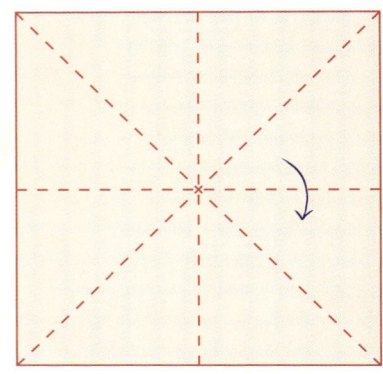
1

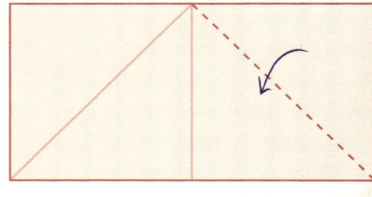
2

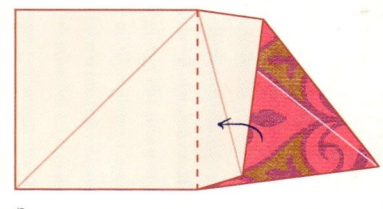
3

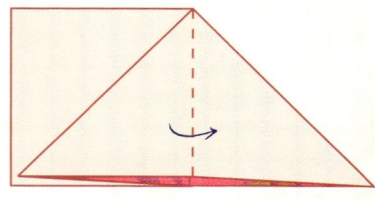
4

jewellery and lucky charms

difficulty

assembly

Pierce right through the two cubes using a needle. Take a headpin and slide on a red bead (or use a pin with a head). Add a small bead cap, slide on the yellow cube and fit a second small bead cap, completing the yellow box.

Using pliers, make a loop with the end of the headpin. Hook this loop on to the loop of the next headpin. Slide a red bead on to the second headpin followed by a large bead cap. Slide on the red cube and fit a final bead cap on its end. Thread on a ring then, using the pliers, close the headpin by forming a loop with the wire. Thread two coated cotton threads through the ring and secure both ends with cord ends and clip together with a fastener.

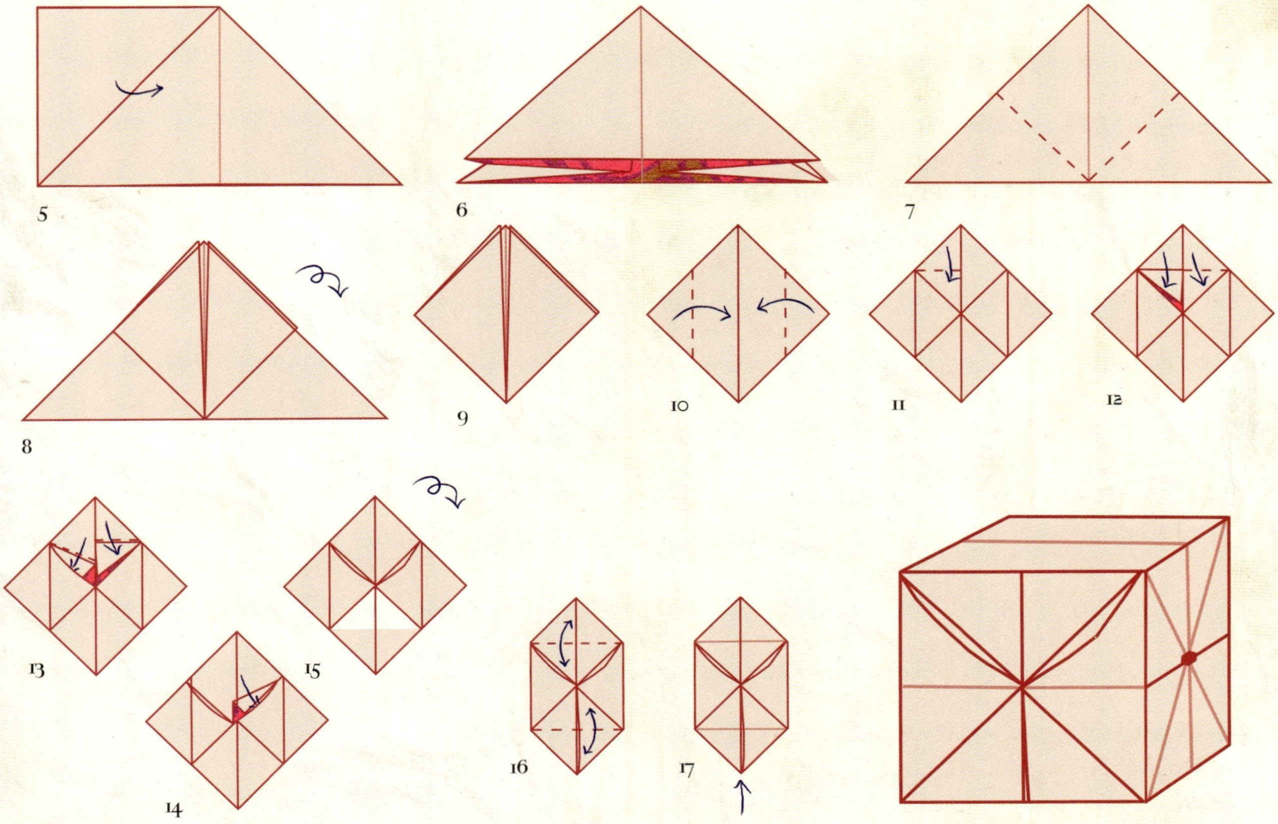

23

hair grips with stars

MATERIALS FOR ONE PAIR OF HAIR GRIPS
1 square of patterned origami paper 5 x 5cm (2 x 2in)
♦ 1 square of plain origami paper 5 x 5cm (2 x 2in) ♦ 2 hair grips

EQUIPMENT
1 paper folder ♦ 1 tube of strong adhesive

folding

1. Cut the two sheets of origami paper in half. Take a rectangle of each type.
2. Fold in half along the dotted line.
3. Fold along the dotted lines as shown.
4. Fold along the dotted lines to form two triangles.
5. Turn the top fold over. Make a quarter turn so that your folding matches the diagram.
6. Overlay the two folds at their centre.
7. Fold the corner of the underneath sheet to the centre and slot it inside the top sheet.
8. Repeat the operation with the opposite corner point.
9. Flip the folding over.
10-11. Repeat steps 7 and 8.

Make the second star from the remaining two rectangles of origami paper.

assembly

Drop a spot of adhesive near the bend in the hair grip and stick a star on top. Hold in place while it dries. Decorate the other hair grip in the same way.

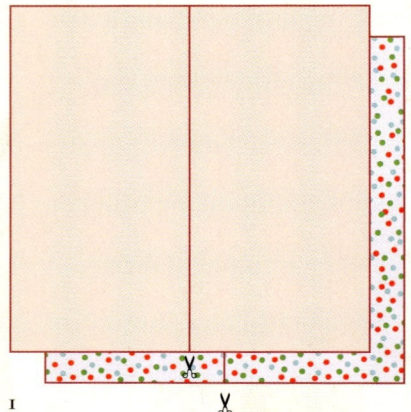

jewellery and lucky charms

difficulty ♦♦

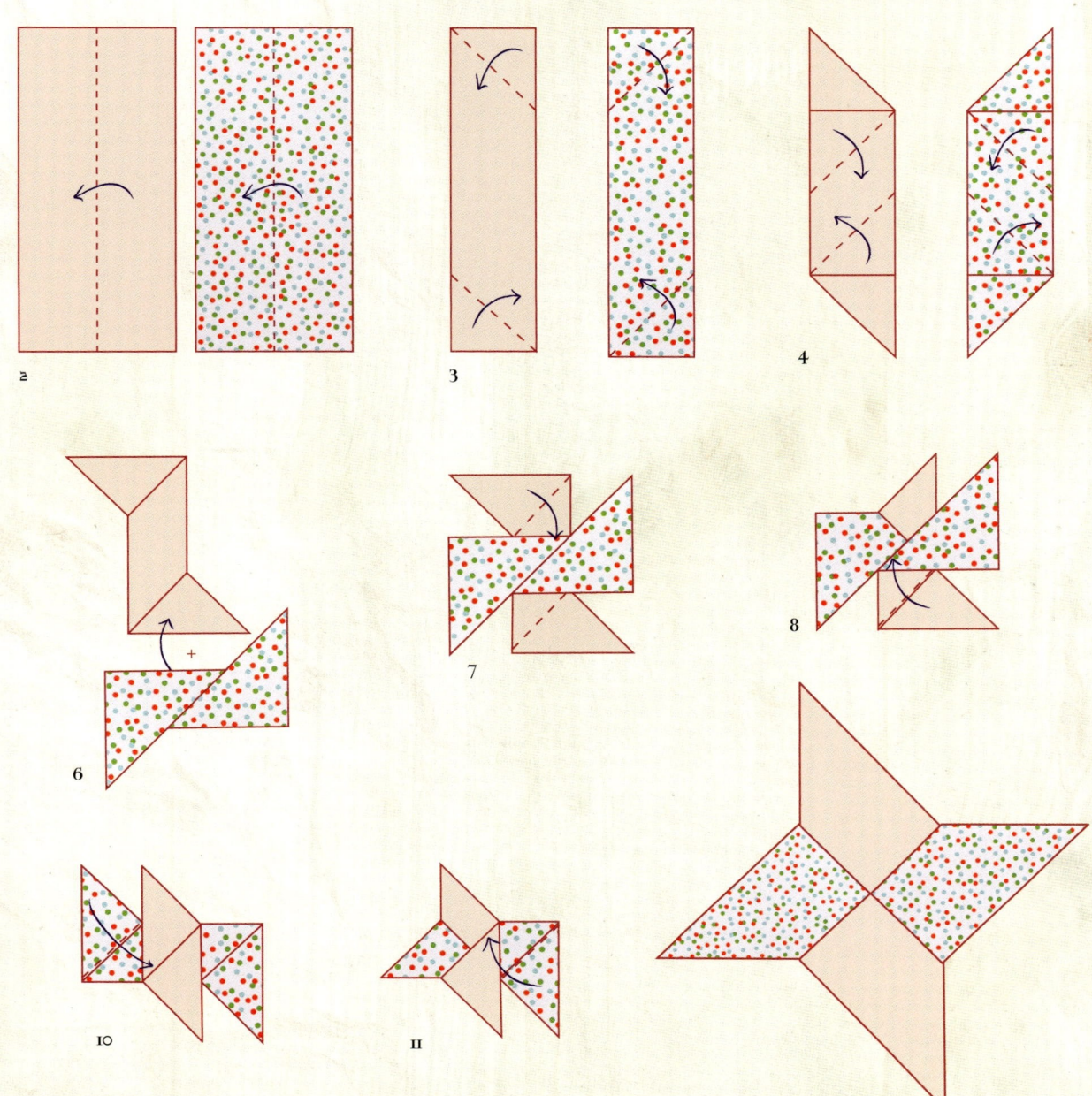

25

jewellery and lucky charms

lucky turtle charm

difficulty

MATERIALS FOR ONE LUCKY CHARM
2 sheets of origami paper 5 x 5cm (2 x 2in) ♦ matching beads ♦ DMC no. 3845 blue stranded cotton thread ♦ lucky charms ♦ matching ribbons ♦ 1 flat ribbon cord end ♦ 1 fastener

EQUIPMENT
1 pair of pliers ♦ 1 sewing needle ♦ 1 tube of adhesive ♦ 1 pair of scissors

folding

1. Score the centre lines and then the diagonals of the square along the dotted lines. Fold downwards along the diagonal fold.
2. Fold along the dotted line.
3. Lift the right point vertically, opening it towards you.
4. Open the sides of the point with the help of the scored creases.
5. Score the fold. Turn the folding over.
6. Repeat steps 3 to 5.
7. Score the folds. Pivot the folding by a quarter turn to the right.
8. Fold along the dotted lines. Score the folds. Unfold.
9. Pick up the bottom point and pull it to the top.
10. Stretch the point upwards to its maximum with the help of the scored creases.
11-12. Flatten the folding into shape as shown.
13. Using a pair of scissors, cut the fold as far as the dotted line. Fold along the dotted lines.
14. Fold the top point of the under sheet towards you. Make an accordion fold with the tip.
15-16. Push the points of the feet inside by inverting the folds.
17. Fold along the dotted lines. Separate the points towards the outside.
18. Fold along the dotted lines.
19. Fold along the dotted line to make a second accordion fold.
20. Turn the folding over and slightly puff out the back of the turtle to make it rounded. Make the second turtle in the same way.

lucky turtle charm (cont.)

assembly

Cut some blue cotton thread. Tie a knot, slide on some beads and secure. Leave a centimetre (about half an inch) space, tie a knot and add a bead. Tie a knot. Glue the thread along the underside of the turtle. Repeat for the second turtle. Add some ribbons, beads and other lucky charms. Fan out the elements for the charm and secure them together in a lucky charm fastener.

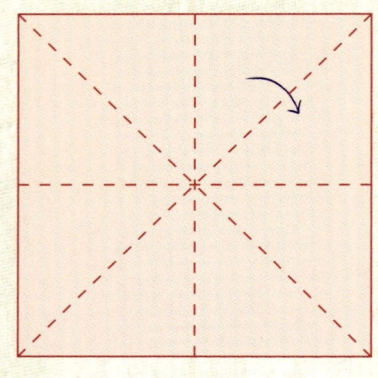
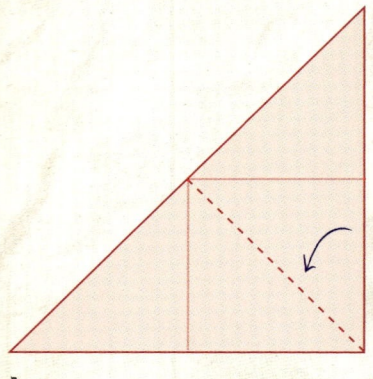

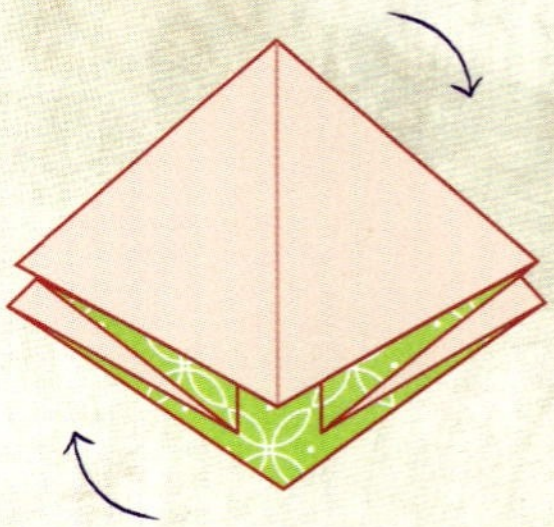

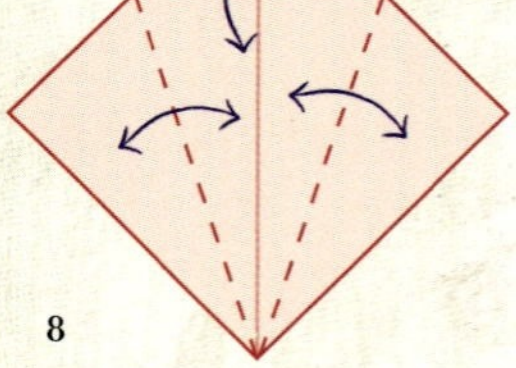

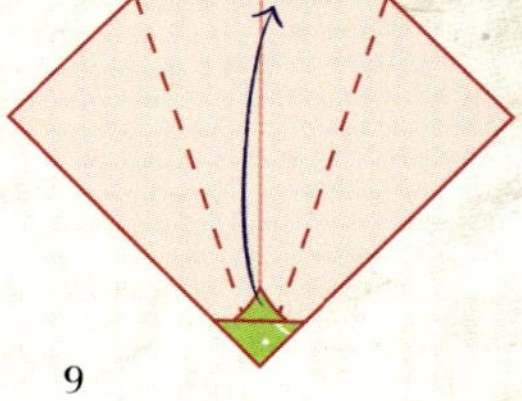

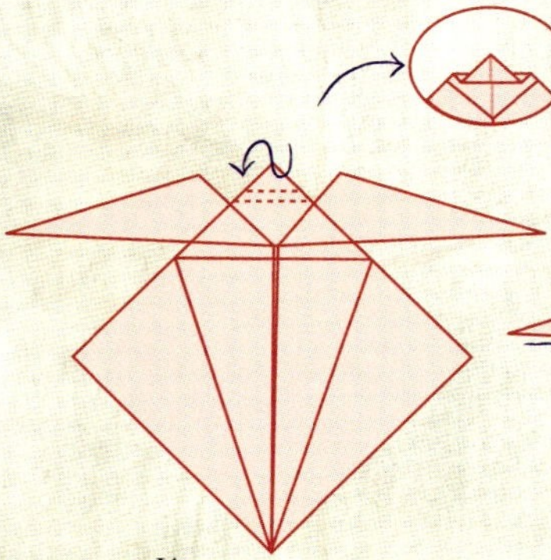

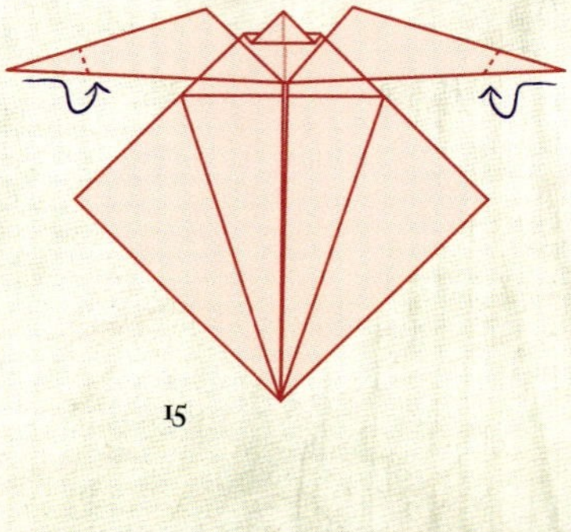

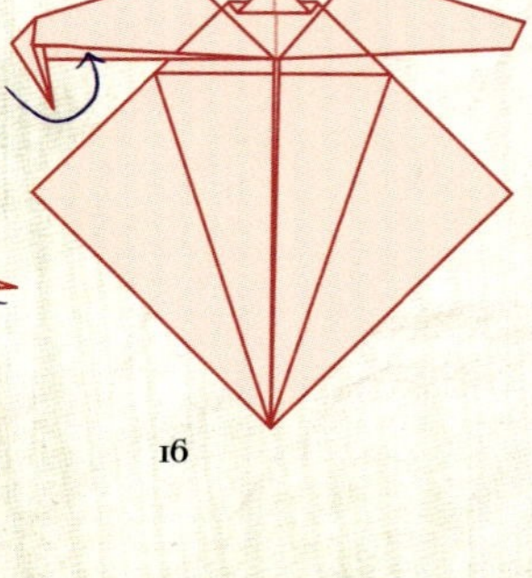

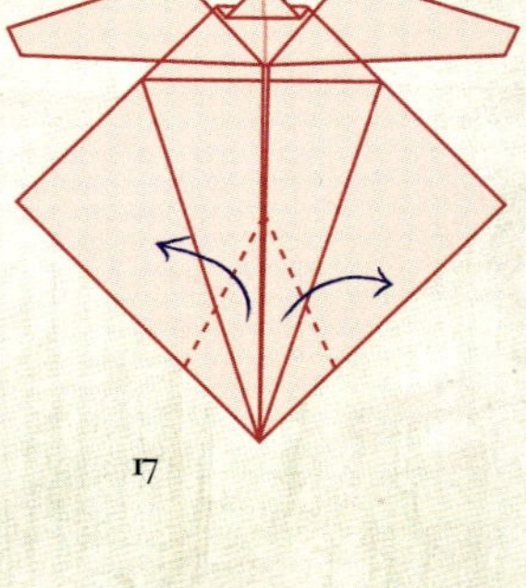

jewellery and lucky charms

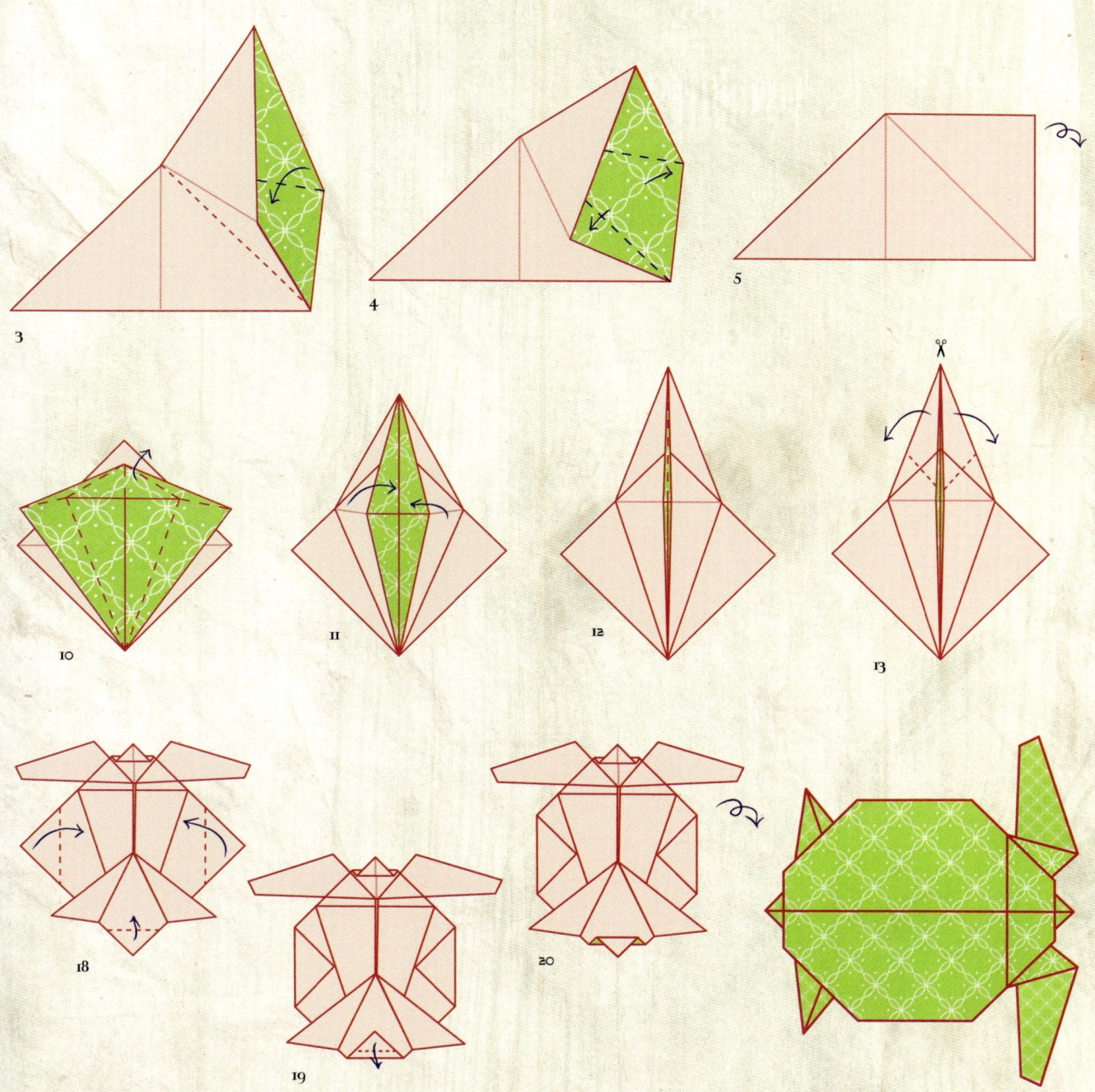

29

jewellery and lucky charms

spring headband difficulty

MATERIALS FOR FOUR CAMELLIAS
4 sheets of origami paper 5 x 5cm (2 x 2in) ♦ 4 sheets of mulberry paper 5 x 5cm (2 x 2in) ♦ 2 sheets of origami paper 4 x 4cm (1½ x 1½in) ♦ turquoise lotus paper 10 x 10cm (4 x 4in) ♦ red beads ♦ red sewing thread ♦ lacquer ♦ 2 headbands

EQUIPMENT
1 pair of pliers ♦ 1 sewing needle ♦ 1 tube of adhesive ♦ 1 pair of scissors ♦ 1 paintbrush

folding

Line each sheet of origami paper with a sheet of coloured mulberry paper in the same size.
1. Score the diagonal folds. Unfold.
2. Fold along the dotted line.
3. Fold along the dotted line again.

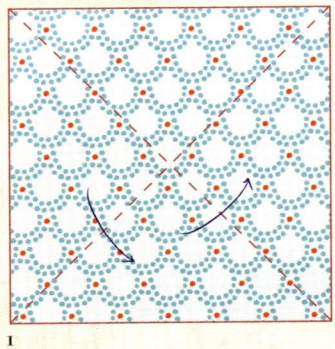
1

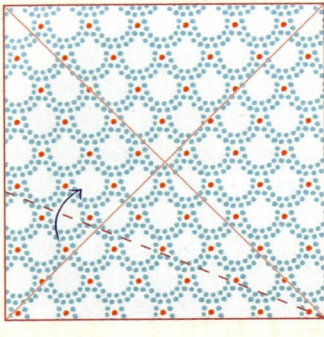
2

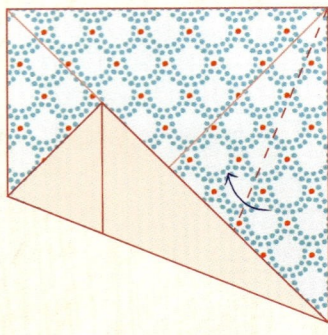
3

spring headband (cont.)

4. Fold along the dotted line.
5. Pull out the bottom corner and open the fold separating it towards you.
6. Flatten the fold to the right.
7. Fold along the dotted line.
8. Fold along the dotted line again.
9. Open the fold towards you and flatten towards the top.
10. Fold along the dotted line.
11. Fold along the dotted line and carefully open the fold towards you.
12. Flatten the new shape making a firm crease then open the fold up entirely, returning the shape to how it was at stage 10.
13. Make the fold again but this time inverting it slightly so the top right-hand point can be tucked under, as shown in diagrams 13-14.
14. Making sure your folds match the diagram, flatten the creases.
15. Fold along the dotted lines. Open the fold towards you, arranging it to tuck under the fold on the right. Flatten.
16-17. Open the heart of the flower folding the inside points along the dotted lines.

assembly

Draw six discs per flower on the turquoise paper. Cut out using a pair of scissors.
 Fold them in half. Glue them overlapping one another to form a flower. Thread a needle with red cotton thread. Tie a knot at one end. Position the blue flower against the origami camellia.
 Sew a red bead through the centre of both flowers from the reverse. Secure with a knot at the back. Repeat in the same way for the other flowers.
 Lacquer with the paintbrush and leave to dry.
 Glue the flowers to a headband.

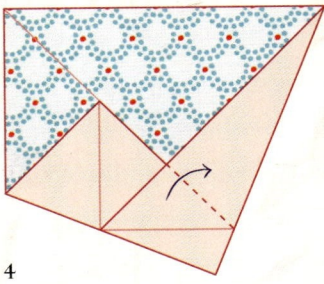
4

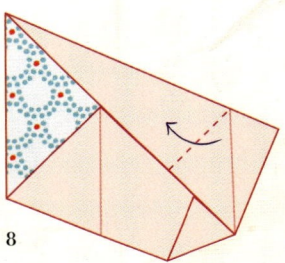
8

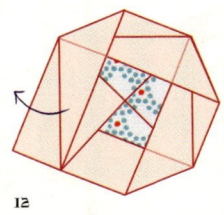
12

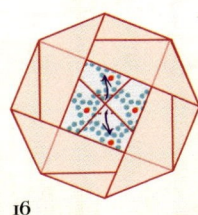
16

jewellery and lucky charms

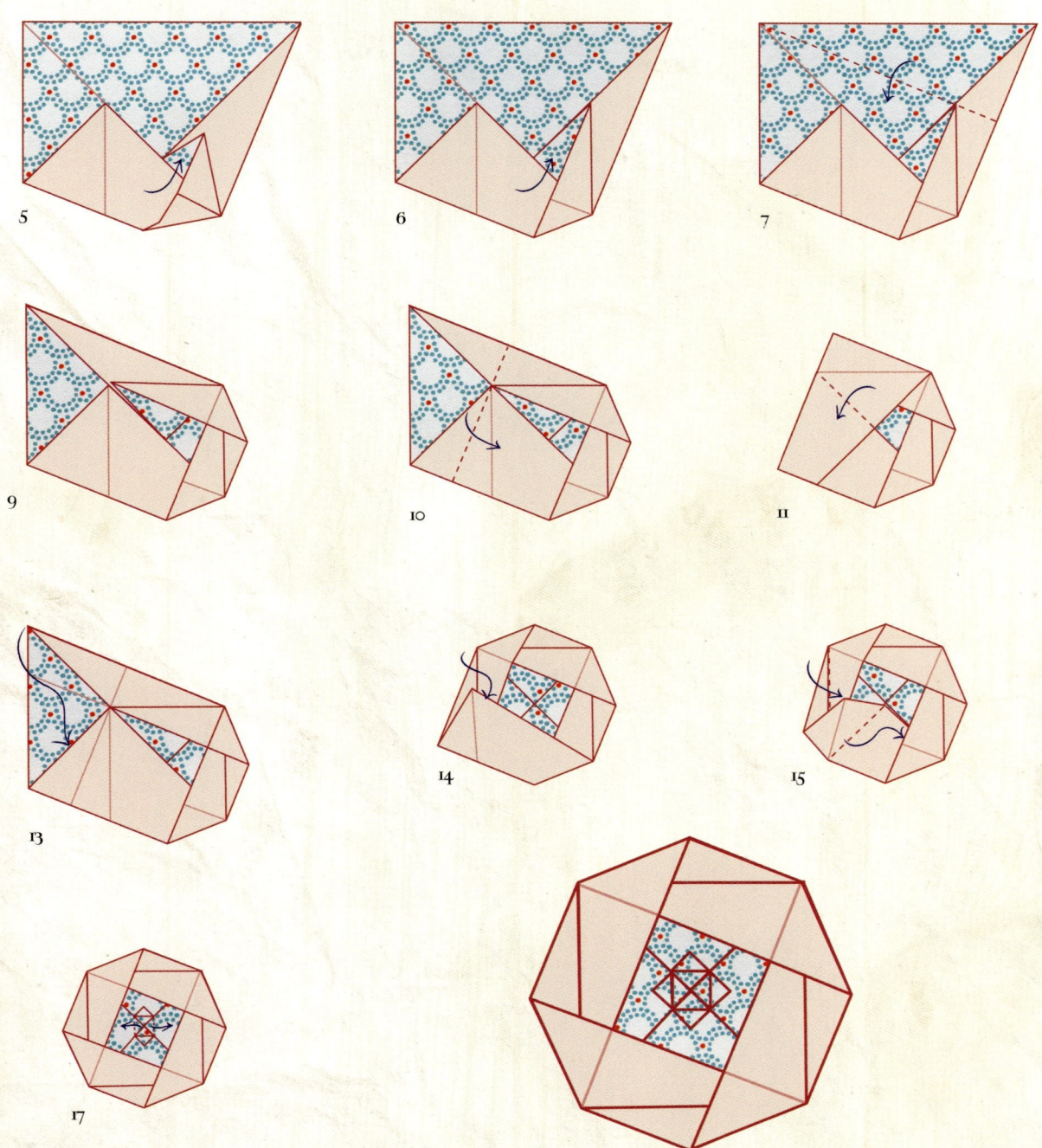

33

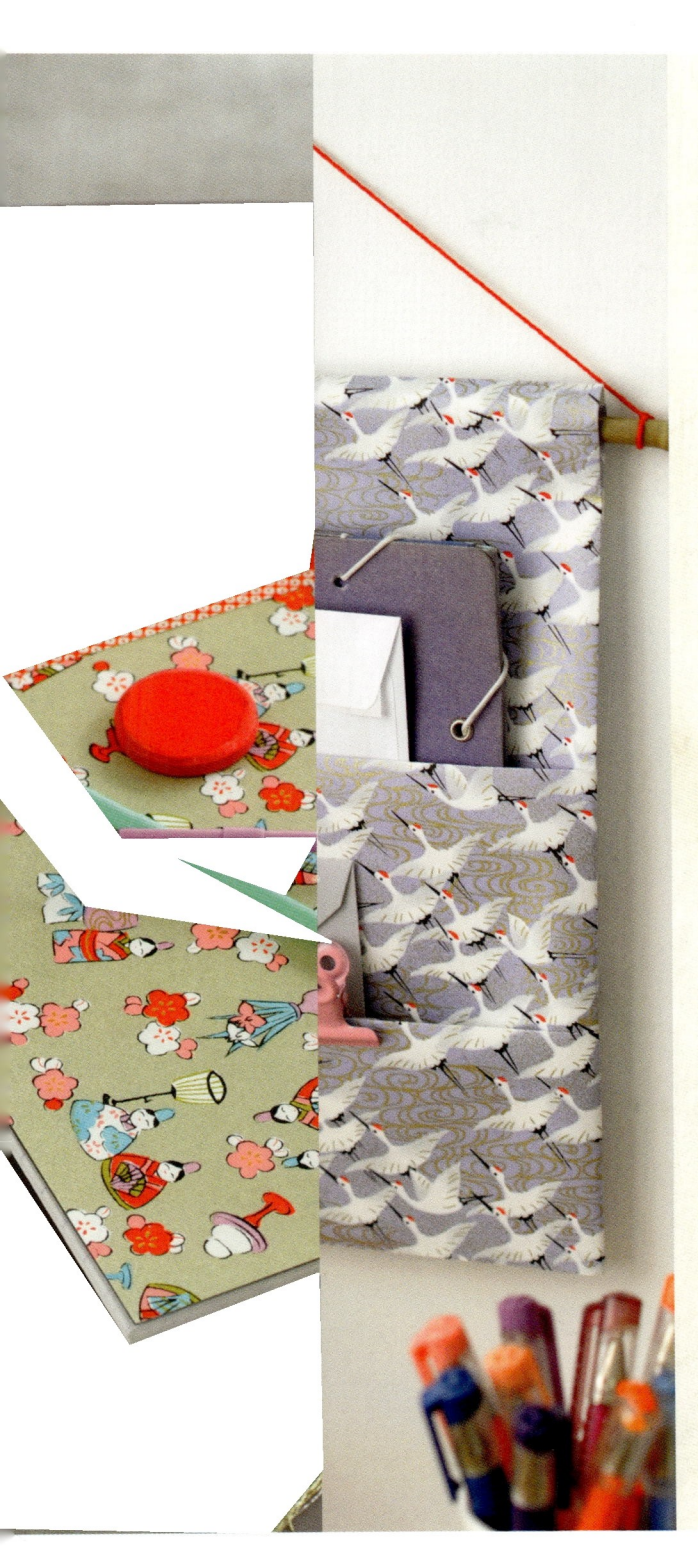

office stationery

bookmark...

stationery holder

office stationery

37

bookmark

MATERIALS FOR TWO BOOKMARKS

2 rectangles of thick, white paper 15 x 5cm (6 x 2in) ♦ 2 rectangles of green, patterned origami paper 15 x 5cm (6 x 2in) ♦ 2 squares of the same paper 3 x 3cm (1¼ x 1¼in) for the flowers ♦ 2 rectangles of red, patterned origami paper 15 x 5cm (6 x 2in) ♦ 2 squares of the same paper 3 x 3cm (1¼ x 1¼in) for the flowers ♦ DMC no. 166 green stranded cotton thread ♦ DMC no. 321 red stranded cotton thread

EQUIPMENT
1 embroidery needle ♦ 1 pair of scissors ♦ 1 pencil ♦ 1 craft knife ♦ 1 cutting mat ♦ 1 ruler ♦ white adhesive ♦ 1 paintbrush for the adhesive ♦ 1 plastic sheet

folding the flower

1. Fold into four.
2. Draw the petal design.
3. Cut out using a pair of scissors.
4. Unfold.
5. Score the folds for the diagonals.

Make a second flower in the same way.

making the bookmarks

Cut out a rectangle 15 x 5cm (6 x 2in) with the craft knife and ruler from a sheet of thick paper. Coat with white adhesive and apply to the reverse of a sheet of origami paper the same size. Smooth out with your hand to remove any bubbles. Cover with a plastic sheet. Place under a very heavy book to flatten the bookmark. Leave to dry overnight. The next day, cover the back of the bookmark with origami paper in the same way. Leave to dry under a press overnight.

ice stationery

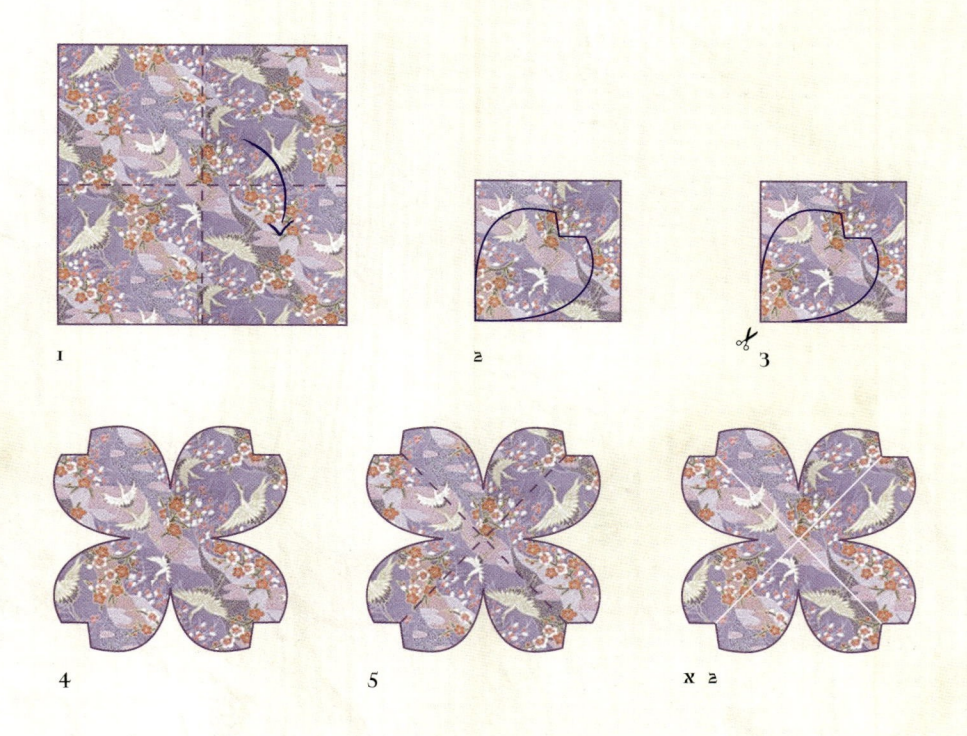

difficulty

1 2 3

4 5 x 2

assembly

Pierce a hole in the centre of one end of the bookmark. Cut a piece of stranded cotton 14cm (5½in) long and fold in half. Slide the loop through the hole. Pass the ends of the thread through the loop just formed and gently pull tight to secure. Glue the cotton threads between the two flowers. Press firmly and leave to dry. Cut out a little heart from paper and glue to the centre of the flowers.

stationery holder

MATERIALS FOR STATIONERY HOLDER
1 rectangle of blue origami paper 30 x 26.8cm (11½ x 10¾in) ◆ 4 rectangles of green origami paper 8.2 x 13cm (3¼ x 5in) ◆ 1 piece of 2mm (⅛in) thick card 5.9 x 5.9cm (2¼ x 2¼in)

EQUIPMENT
1 pencil ◆ 1 paper folder ◆ 1 craft knife ◆ 1 cutting mat ◆ 1 ruler ◆ 1 tube of adhesive

folding

1. Using a pencil, measure and mark out the positions of the folds to be made.
2. Fold over the second fold.
3. Score the fold at the bottom and unfold. Measure and mark the positions of the folds to be made using a pencil.
4. Fold the bottom left corner, unfold.
5. Fold along the dotted line.
6. Fold the bottom left corner along the dotted line and unfold. Open the folding.

office stationery

difficulty ♦♦♦

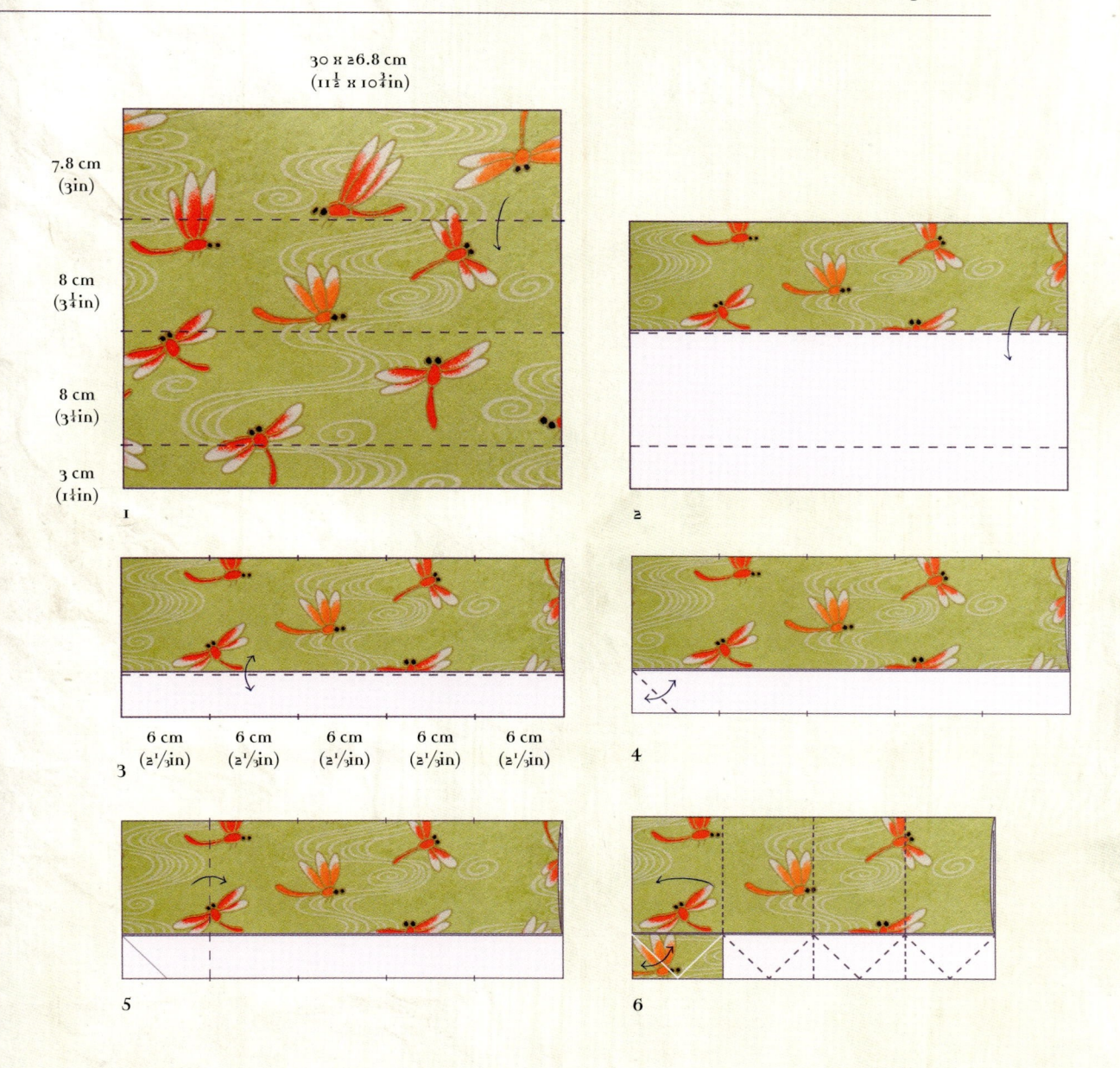

30 x 26.8 cm
(11½ x 10¾in)

7.8 cm
(3in)

8 cm
(3¼in)

8 cm
(3¼in)

3 cm
(1¼in)

1

2

6 cm   6 cm   6 cm   6 cm   6 cm
(2⅓in)   (2⅓in)   (2⅓in)   (2⅓in)   (2⅓in)

3

4

5

6

41

stationery holder (cont.)

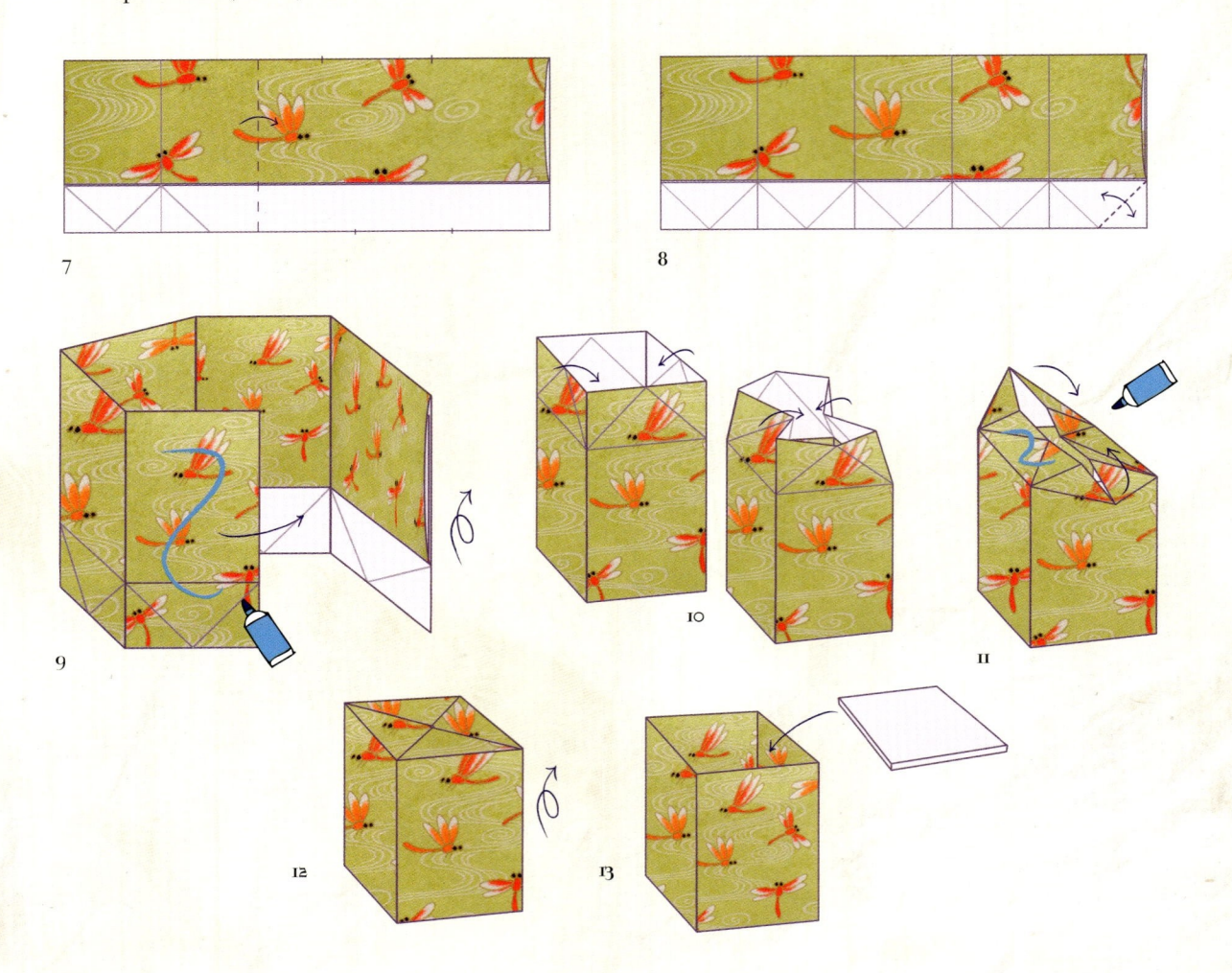

7

8

9

10

11

12

13

7. Fold along the dotted line. Repeat steps 5 and 6.
8. Repeat the preceding steps for each pencil mark. Score the fold of the bottom right corner.
9. Assemble the pencil holder. Glue and hold in place while the adhesive dries. Turn the shape over.
10. Turn in two sides in the direction of the arrows to close the holder.
11. Flatten. Add a spot of glue.
12. Turn in the two other points and hold in place while the adhesive dries.
13. Turn the holder over. Slip some card into the holder and position it on the bottom to add stability to the holder.

office stationery

pockets

1. Fold the flap along the dotted line.
2. Mark the points for the folds at the places indicated. Turn the bottom flap to the rear.
3. Score all the folds. Assemble the folding. Push in the folds at the sides to make a pocket. Glue the bottom and the side to close up the pocket.
4. Make four pockets of different heights.
5. Glue the pockets to the pen holder. Hold in place while the adhesive dries.

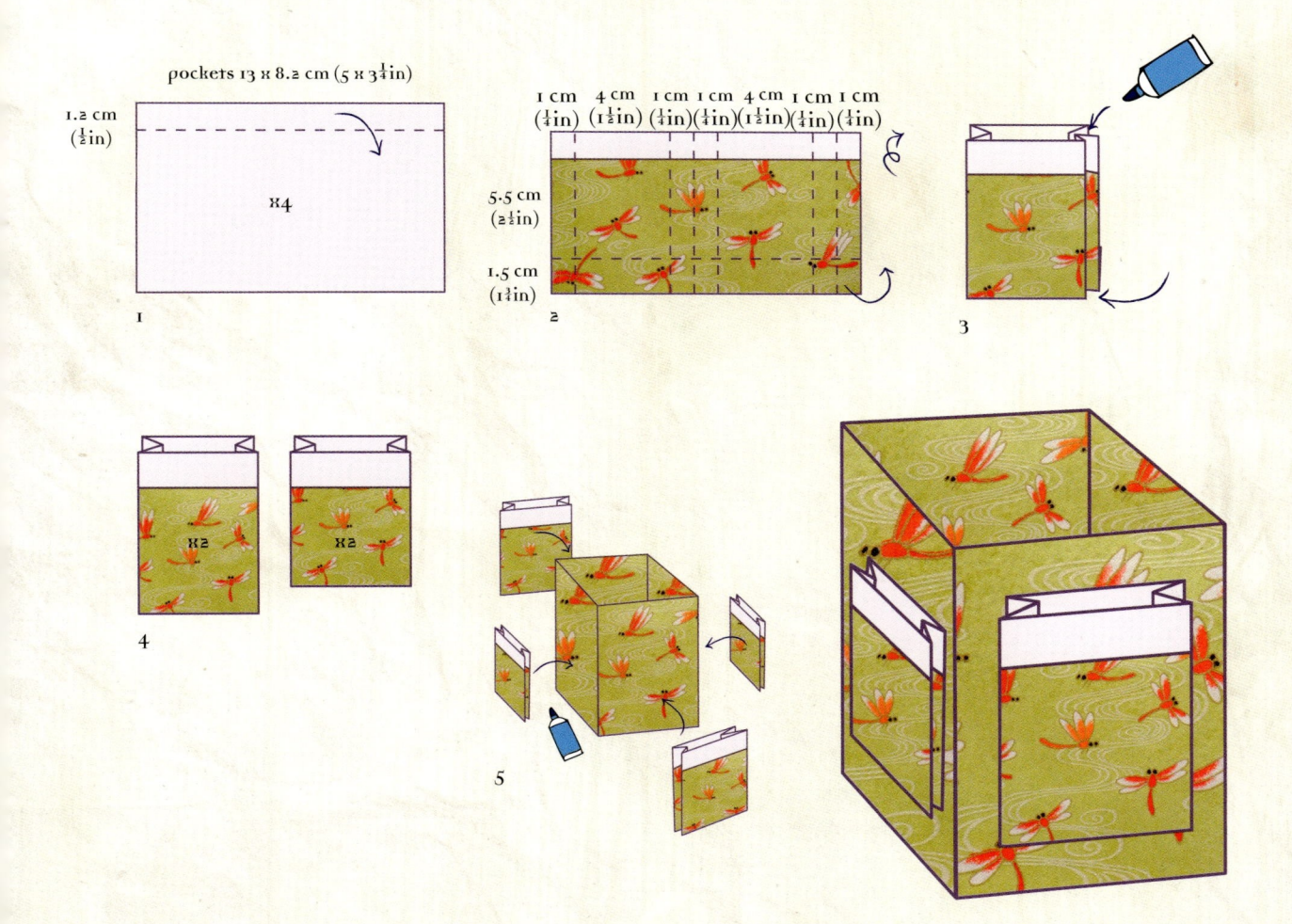

pockets 13 x 8.2 cm (5 x 3¼ in)

1.2 cm (½ in)

x4

1 cm 4 cm 1 cm 1 cm 4 cm 1 cm 1 cm
(¼in) (1½in) (¼in)(¼in)(1½in)(¼in)(¼in)

5.5 cm (2¼ in)

1.5 cm (1¾ in)

43

love cards

drawing pads

office stationery

love cards

MATERIALS FOR TWO CARDS
1 green card 16 x 16cm (6¼ x 6¼in) when folded ♦ 1 red card 16 x 16cm (6¼ x 6¼in) when folded ♦ 6 rectangles of different patterned origami papers 16 x 5cm (6¼ x 2in) ♦ 2 scraps of patterned origami paper

EQUIPMENT
1 paper folder ♦ 1 pair of scissors ♦ 1 pencil ♦ 1 craft knife ♦ 1 cutting mat ♦ 1 ruler ♦ 1 tube of adhesive

making the cards

Butterfly card
Trace the butterfly motifs on to the reverse side of the front of the folded green card. Cut out with the craft knife, leaving the central strips. Fold the butterflies along the dotted lines.

Glue three rectangular strips of origami paper on the inside cover of the card so that the patterned pieces show through the front of the card. Cut out two extra butterflies from the scraps of patterned origami paper. Fold them along the dotted lines and glue to the front of the card as show in the photograph.

Adjust the wings of the butterflies to give a three-dimensional effect.

Heart card
Trace the motifs for the hearts on to the reverse side of the front of the folded red card. Cut out with the craft knife. Fold the hearts along the dotted lines. Open the card and glue on three strips of origami paper to the inside cover so that the patterns show through on the front.

Adjust the hearts so that they stand out on the front of the card.

office stationery

difficulty ◆

butterfly card shapes: 16 x 16 cm (when folded)

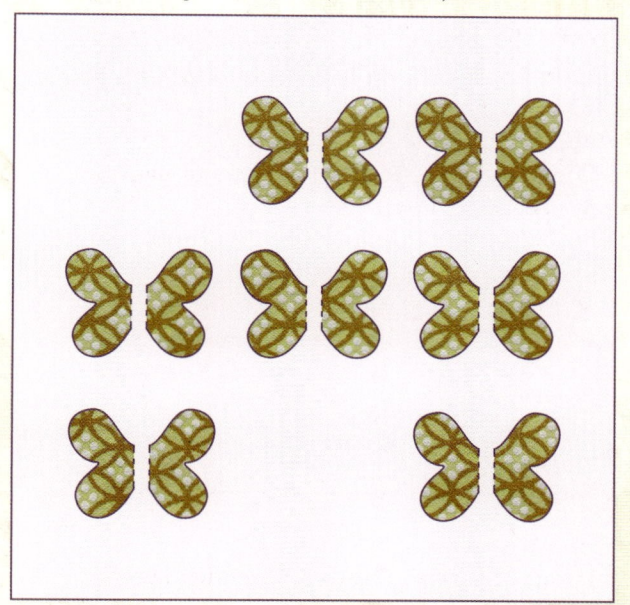

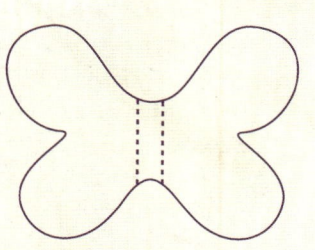

butterfly at actual size

enlarge to 200%

heart card shapes: 16 x 16 cm (when folded)

heart at actual size

enlarge to 200%

47

drawing pads

MATERIALS FOR ONE PAD

2 rectangles of 270gsm (182lbs) red Maya paper 21 x 13.5cm (8¼ x 5¼in)
♦ 2 rectangles of red and gold patterned paper 21 x 13.5cm (8¼ x 5¼in)
♦ 1 rectangle of matching origami paper 13.5 x 5cm (5¼ x 2in)
♦ 1 strip of matching origami paper 13.5 x 0.5cm (5¼ x ¼in)
♦ 15 sheets of thin, light beige paper 21 x 13.5cm (8¼ x 5¼in)
♦ scraps of red and gold patterned paper ♦ DMC 'metal effect' grey anthracite no. E317 stranded cotton thread ♦ 1 scrap of card

EQUIPMENT

1 paper folder ♦ 1 embroidery needle ♦ 1 pair of scissors ♦ 1 can of spray adhesive ♦ 1 tube of adhesive ♦ 1 pencil ♦ 1 craft knife ♦ 1 cutting mat ♦ 1 ruler ♦ 1 compass

making the drawing pads

Cut the inside sheets to the sizes stated. Cut the cover and the back of the pad from Maya paper and red and gold patterned paper.

Apply spray adhesive to the Maya paper and place the red and gold paper on top. Glue a rectangle of origami paper near the fold of the cover. Add a strip of matching origami paper. Cover the back of the pad in the same way. Mark the position of the holes with a pencil and place a piece of card under the cover as shown. Pierce with an embroidery needle. Pierce the inside pages and the back of the pad in the same way.

Assemble the components of the pad. Thread a needle with three strands of anthracite metallic thread to prepare for the binding. To make the binding, follow the diagram opposite.

1. Thread the needle through the second hole from the bottom, entering from the back of the pad. Pass the thread through the pad and the inside pages and up through the corresponding hole above.
2. Pass the thread around the spine and back through the same hole.
3. Pulling the thread along the top of the pad, thread it through to the top of the first hole and pass the needle through the pages and out of the bottom.
4. From the bottom hole, pass the thread around the spine and thread it back through the top of the first hole for the second time.
5. This time pass the thread up around the outside edge of the pad and thread back into the first hole for a third time.

office stationery

difficulty ♦♦

6. Pass the thread along the base to the second hole from the bottom.
7. Bring the thread up through the second hole and sew over to the third hole.
8. From the bottom of the third hole, pass the thread around the spine and back into the third hole a second time.
9. Pass the thread along the base of the pad and up through the last hole.
10. Pass the thread around the spine and then thread back through the bottom hole.
11. From the top of the last hole, pass the thread round the spine once more and then back through the bottom hole.
12. Pass the thread over to the second hole from the top, as shown.
13. Bring the thread out of the base of the pad. Tie firmly and cut the excess thread.

Using the same paper as the front cover, draw two circles 3cm (1¼in) in diameter on the reverse side of the sheet. Cut out. On a matching piece of origami paper draw four circles 3cm (1¼in) in diameter on the reverse of the sheet. Cut out.

Cut five pieces of anthracite metallic thread around 15cm (6in) long. Open the pad and mark the centre of the bottom edge. Apply a dot of adhesive and attach the ends of the metallic thread. Passing the metallic thread between them, glue two discs one on top of the other. Hold in place while the adhesive dries. Repeat for the back of the pad.

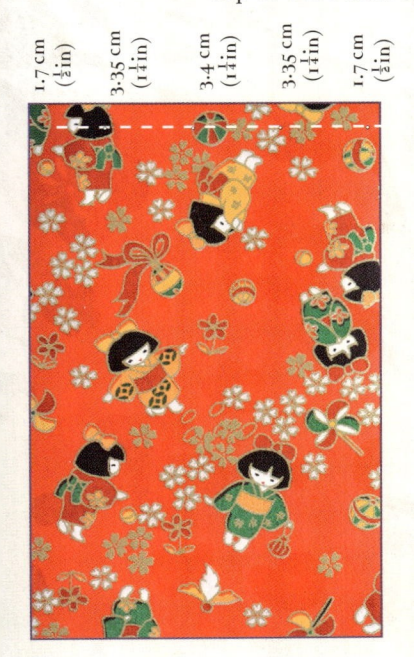

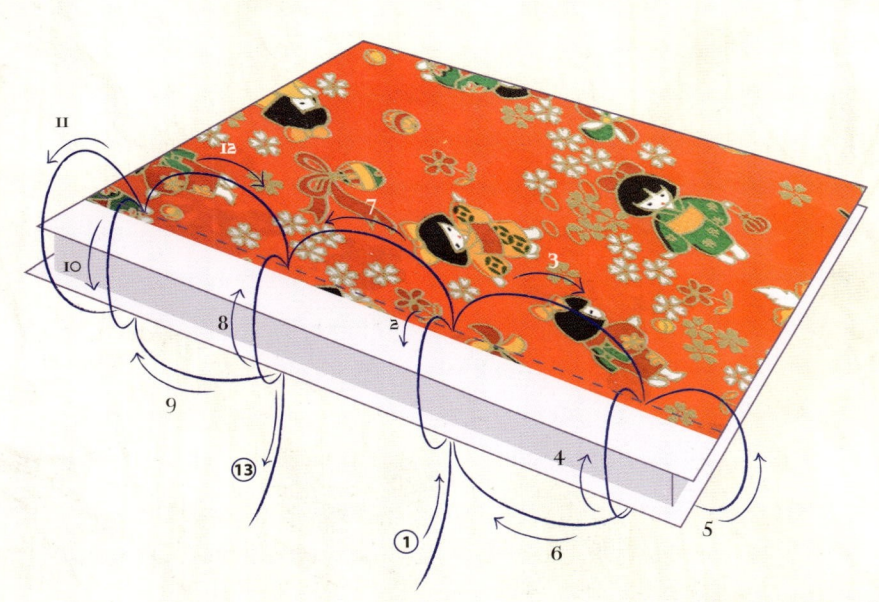

housekeeping book

office stationery

wall tidy

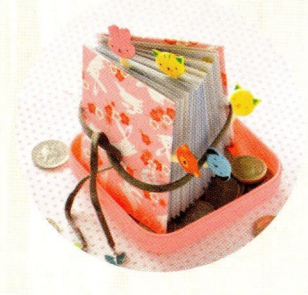

housekeeping book

MATERIALS FOR ONE HOUSEKEEPING BOOK
2 rectangles of 1mm thick white card 7.3 x 10.3cm (2¾ x 4in)
♦ 2 sheets of origami paper 15 x 15cm 6 x 6in) ♦ 4 sheets of white craft paper
♦ white adhesive ♦ 30cm (11¾in) of ribbon ♦ 2 lucky charms ♦ sewing thread

EQUIPMENT
1 paper folder ♦ 1 paintbrush ♦ 1 sewing needle ♦ 1 pair of scissors ♦ 1 pencil
♦ 1 craft knife ♦ 1 cutting mat ♦ 1 ruler ♦ 1 plastic sheet

making the housekeeping book

1. Cut the cards and the origami paper sheets to size. Cut the corners of the sheets of origami paper as shown in the diagram. Place a sheet face down on the work surface, which is covered with a plastic sheet. Paint white adhesive over it using a paintbrush. Place the white card on top. Smooth out any bubbles with your hands.
2. Spread white adhesive on the excess paper using a paintbrush. Turn over the edges. Smooth out any bubbles with your hands. Leave to dry and place under a press overnight. Make the back of the housekeeping book in the same way.
3. Cut the sheets of white craft paper into strips of 10.5 x 29.7cm (4¼ x 11¾in) and fold them like an accordion. Glue the ends to the back of the card covers. Leave to dry
4. Fold up the housekeeping book again. Sew lucky charms to the ends of a ribbon. Wind the ribbon around the book and tie to close it.

office stationery

difficulty ●●

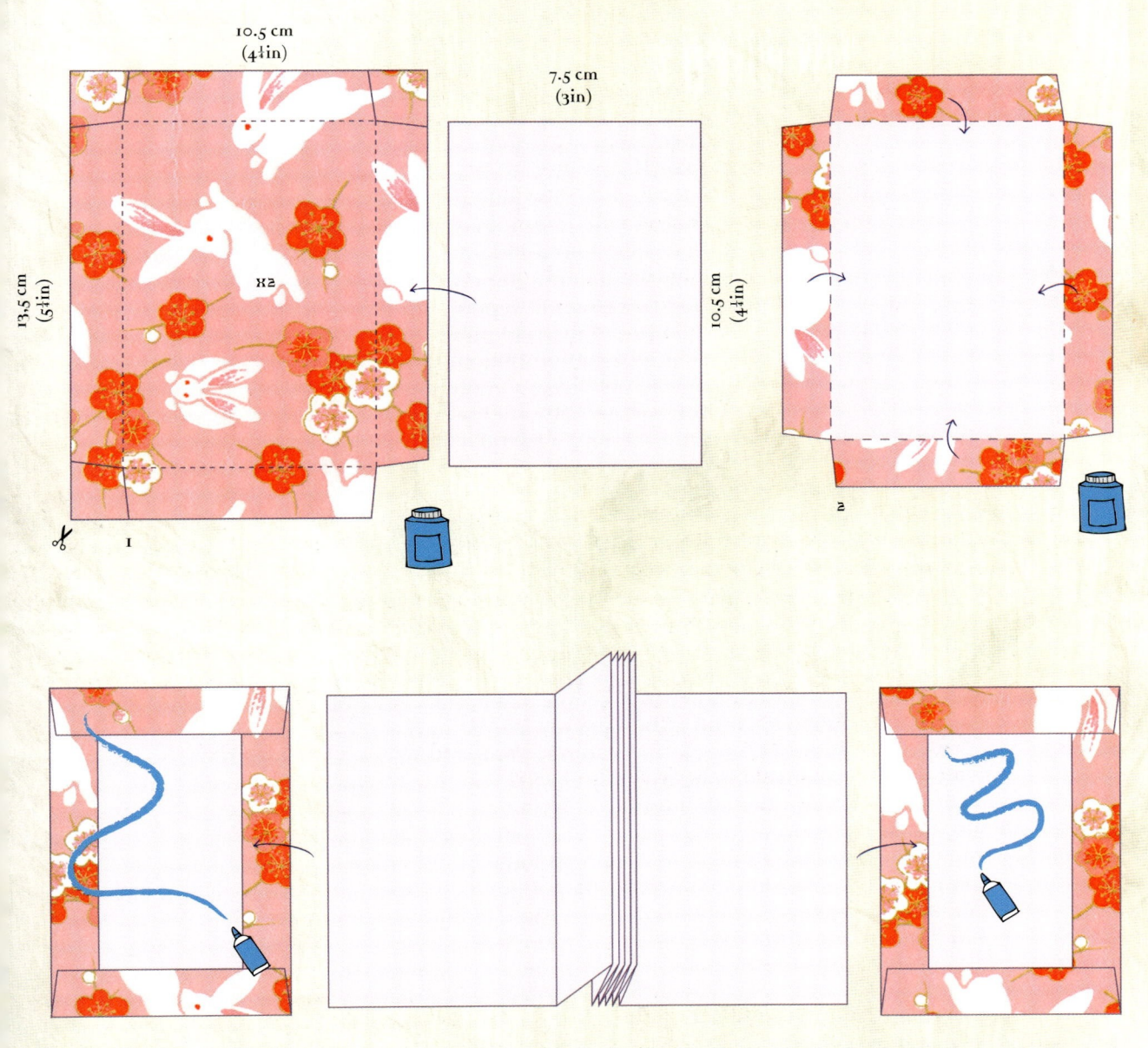

10.5 cm (4¼in)

7.5 cm (3in)

13.5 cm (5¼in)

10.5 cm (4¼in)

x2

1

2

3

wall tidy

MATERIALS FOR THE WALL TIDY
1 sheet of origami paper 60 x 42cm (23½ x 16½in)
♦ 1 piece of bamboo 35cm (13¾in) long ♦ 50cm (19¾in) of red cord
♦ 1 lucky charm ♦ DMC no. 321 red stranded cotton thread
♦ 1 tube of adhesive

EQUIPMENT
1 paper folder ♦ 1 embroidery needle ♦ 1 pair of scissors
♦ 1 pencil ♦ 1 ruler

folding

1. Fold along the dotted line and score the fold.
2. Fold along the dotted line.
3. Turn the entire folding over.
4. Fold along the dotted line.
5. Turn the entire folding over.
6. Fold along the dotted line.
7. Fold the corners along the dotted lines.
8. Score the folds along the dotted lines. Apply a line of adhesive. Fold and hold in place while the adhesive dries.
9. Score the fold along the dotted line. Apply a line of adhesive as close as possible to the top edge of the sheet. Fold and hold in place while the adhesive dries. Turn the folding over.

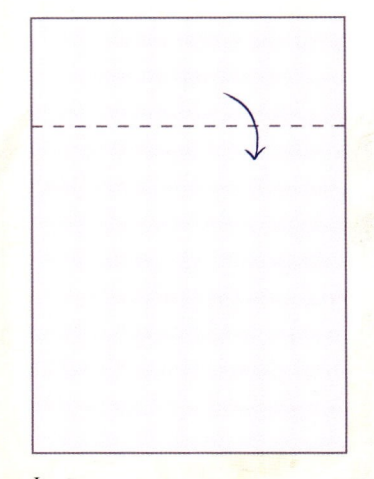

assembly

Slide a piece of bamboo into the top fold. Tie the red cord to the ends of the bamboo.

Draw a mark at the bottom of the wall tidy to mark the centre. Pierce a hole in it using a sewing needle. Fold three strands of red stranded cotton in half. Slide the loop into the hole, pass the ends of the thread into the loop and gently pull tight. Decorate with a lucky charm.

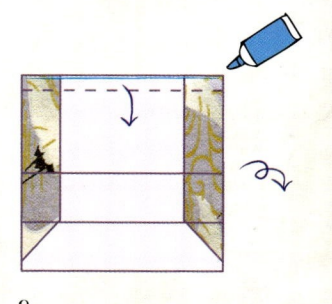

office stationery

difficulty ●●

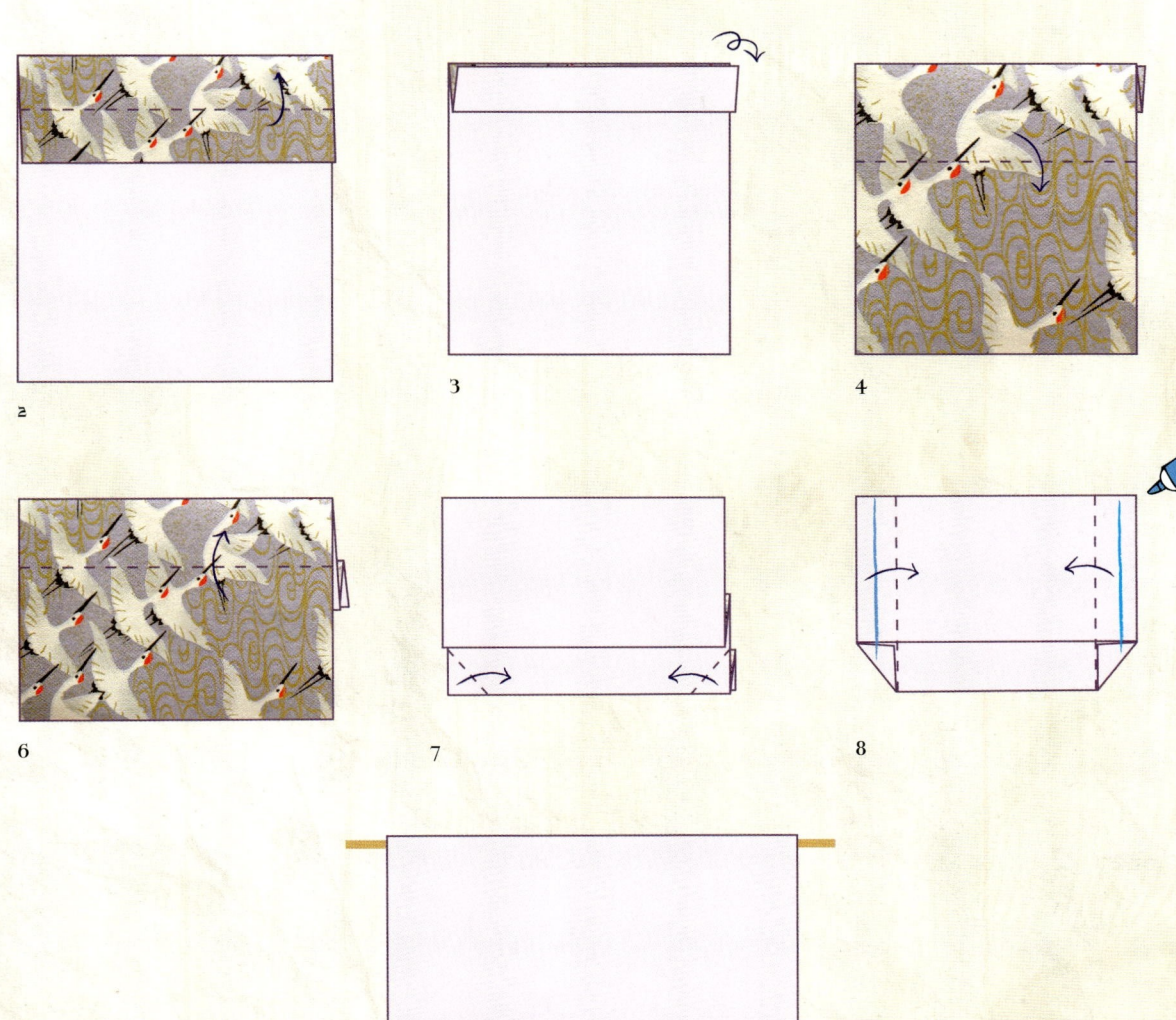

2

3

4

6

7

8

55

56

decorations for the home

decorations for the home

japanese floral lampshade   difficulty ◆

MATERIALS
1 sheet of A3 patterned origami paper 21 x 29.7cm (8¼ x 11¾in) ◆ 1 sheet of A4 fuchsia pink Nepalese banana paper 21 x 29.7cm (8¼ x 11¾in) ◆ 1 sheet of A4 red Nepalese banana paper 21 x 29.7cm (8¼ x 11¾in) ◆ 1 strip of red corrugated card 5 x 39cm (2 x 15¼in) ◆ 1 strip of red corrugated card 4 x 29cm (1½ x 11½in) ◆ DMC no. 321 red stranded cotton thread ◆ 1 sheet of tracing paper ◆ craft tape ◆ 1 Japanese lampshade

EQUIPMENT
1 pencil ◆ 1 pair of scissors ◆ 1 tube of adhesive ◆ 1 craft knife ◆ 1 ruler ◆ 1 cutting mat

assembly

Trace the shape of the flower. Transfer twice on to the reverse of a piece of origami paper, and again on to the sheet of red Nepalese banana paper and then again on to the sheet of fuchsia pink Nepalese banana paper. Using scissors, cut out the six flowers and glue to the lampshade.

Cut out the two strips of red corrugated card. Assemble into a ring with the corrugation on the inside. Close up by securing with some craft tape. Cover with patterned origami paper in the same size. Glue. Leave to dry. Assemble the lampshade and glue the flowers on to it. Glue a ring of corrugated card around each of the openings of the lampshade. Make a tassel with some red stranded cotton and attach to the lampshade.

enlarge to 200%
height: 13.5cm (5¼in)

59

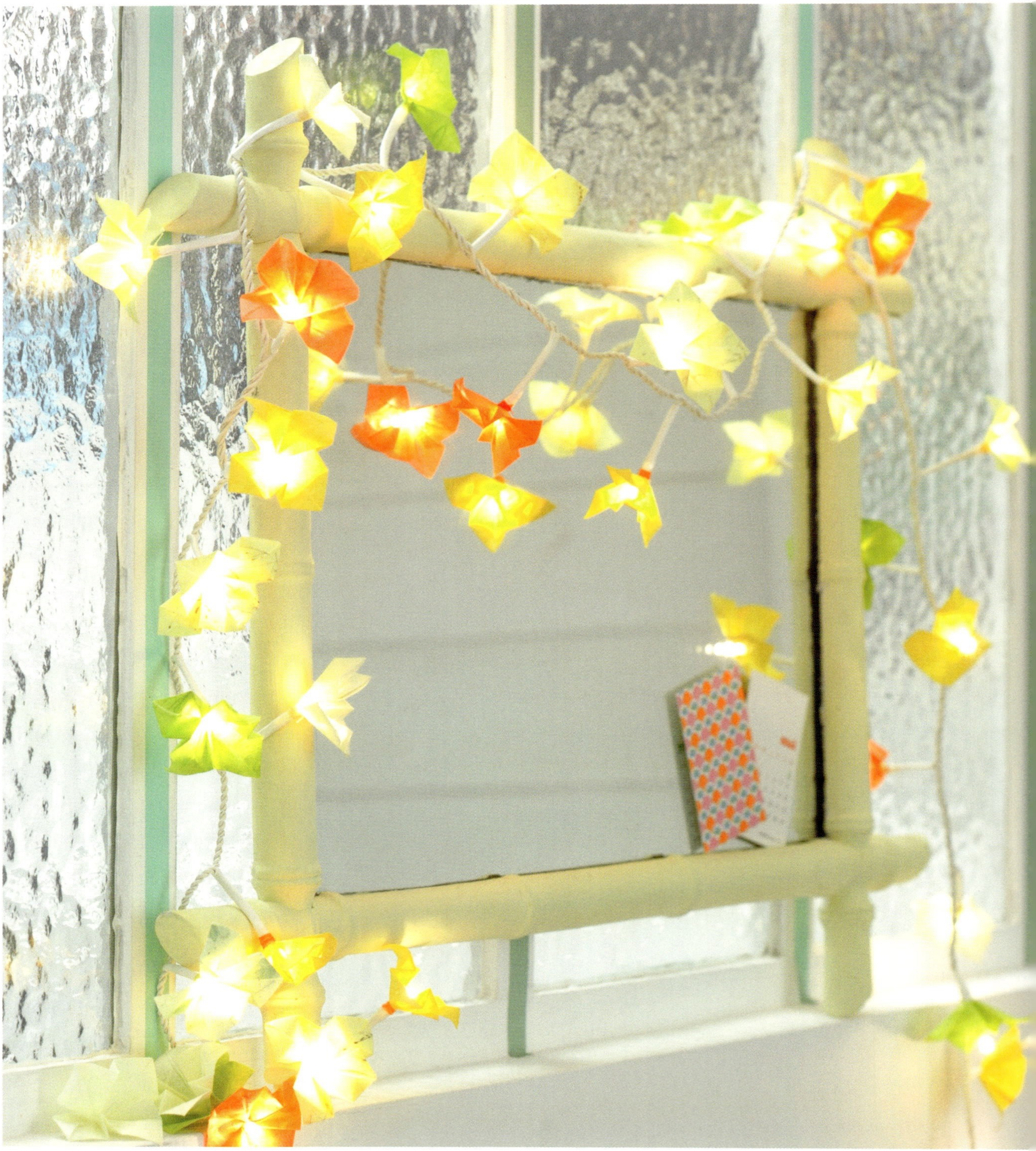

decorations for the home

string of lights

difficulty ♦♦

MATERIALS FOR ONE STRING OF LIGHTS
15 squares of yellow mulberry paper 5 x 5cm (2 x 2in) ♦ 15 squares of pale yellow mulberry paper 5 x 5cm (2 x 2in) ♦ 15 squares of white mulberry paper 5 x 5cm (2 x 2in) ♦ 15 squares of orange mulberry paper 5 x 5cm (2 x 2in) ♦ 15 squares of lime green mulberry paper 5 x 5cm (2 x 2in) ♦ 1 string of LED electric light bulbs ♦ sewing thread in matching colours

EQUIPMENT
1 paper folder ♦ 1 pair of scissors ♦ 1 pencil

folding

1. Fold each square into four. Unfold. Fold the two left-hand points over to the centre along the dotted lines.
2. Fold the two other points over to the centre.
3. Pivot the paper by a quarter turn to the right.

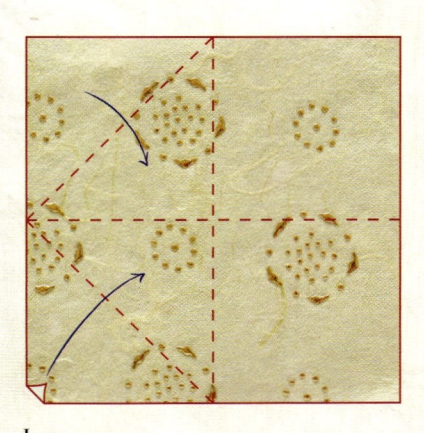

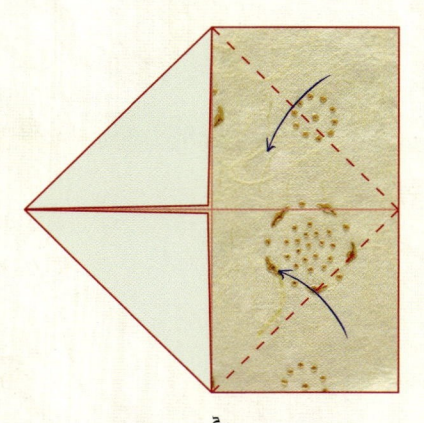

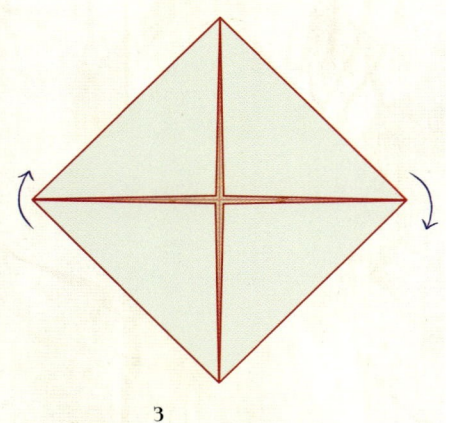

string of lights (cont.)

4. Fold the centre lines along the dotted lines. Unfold. Fold in half to the rear.
5. Score the fold along the dotted line.
6. Lift the right point vertically, opening it towards you with the help of the scored creases.
7. Flatten, score the fold. Turn the left point back towards the right along the dotted line.
8. Turn the left point to the right again along the dotted line. Repeat steps 3 to 5.
9. Score the folds.
10. Fold along the dotted line and unfold.
11. Open the point vertically with the help of the scored creases.
12. Flatten and score the folds.

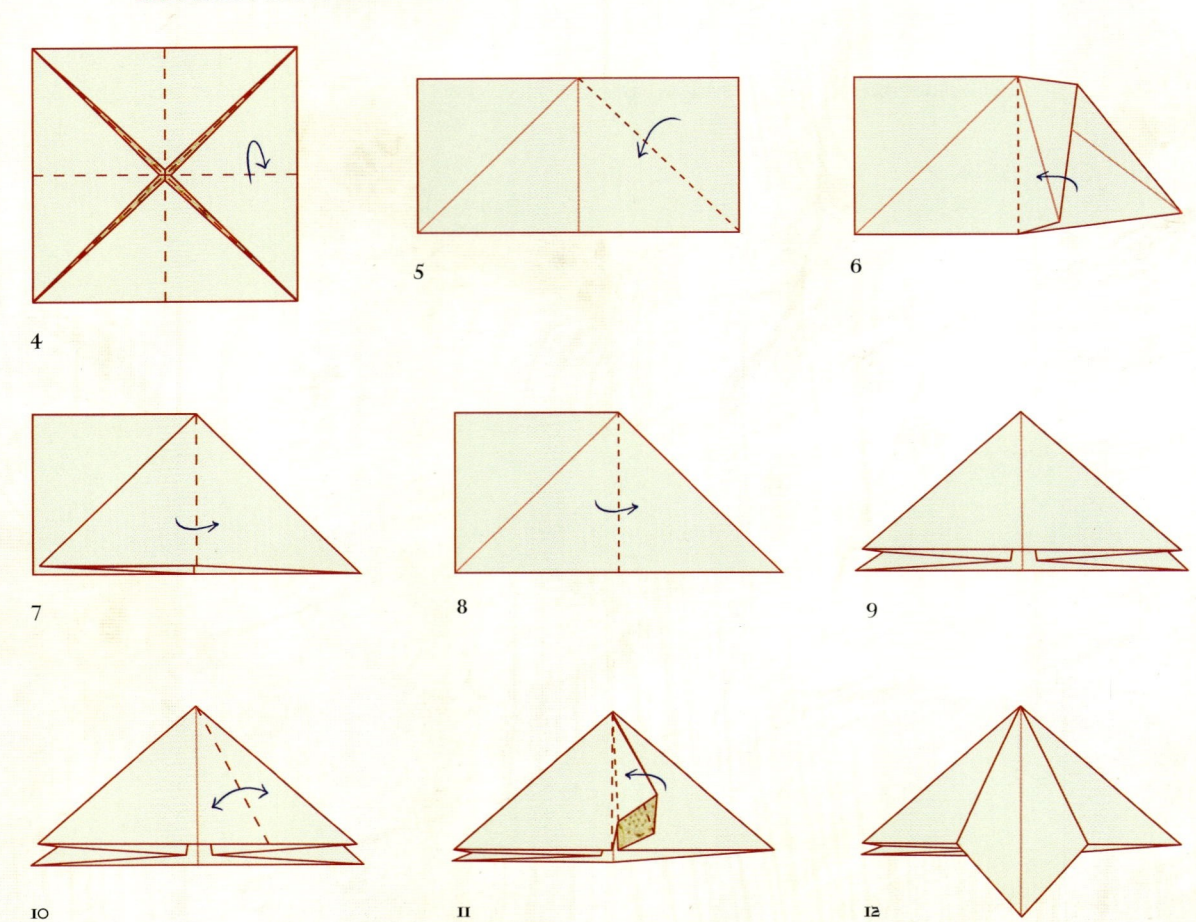

decorations for the home

13. Turn the right sheet towards the left along the dotted line.
14. Repeat steps 10 to 12 with the right sheet. Repeat steps 10 to 12 for the remaning corners.
15. Flatten the whole folding and pivot by 180°.
16. Take a pencil and roll the top of the petal around it to give a rounded edge.
17. Open the flower and shape all the petals. Make the other flowers in the same way.

assembly

Cut off the points at the base of the flowers. Slide an LED bulb from the string of lights into each flower. Choose some sewing thread to match the flowers. Wrap the thread around the base of each flower. Pull tight, tie a knot and cut off the excess thread. Use different coloured paper on each bulb to create a varied colour effect.

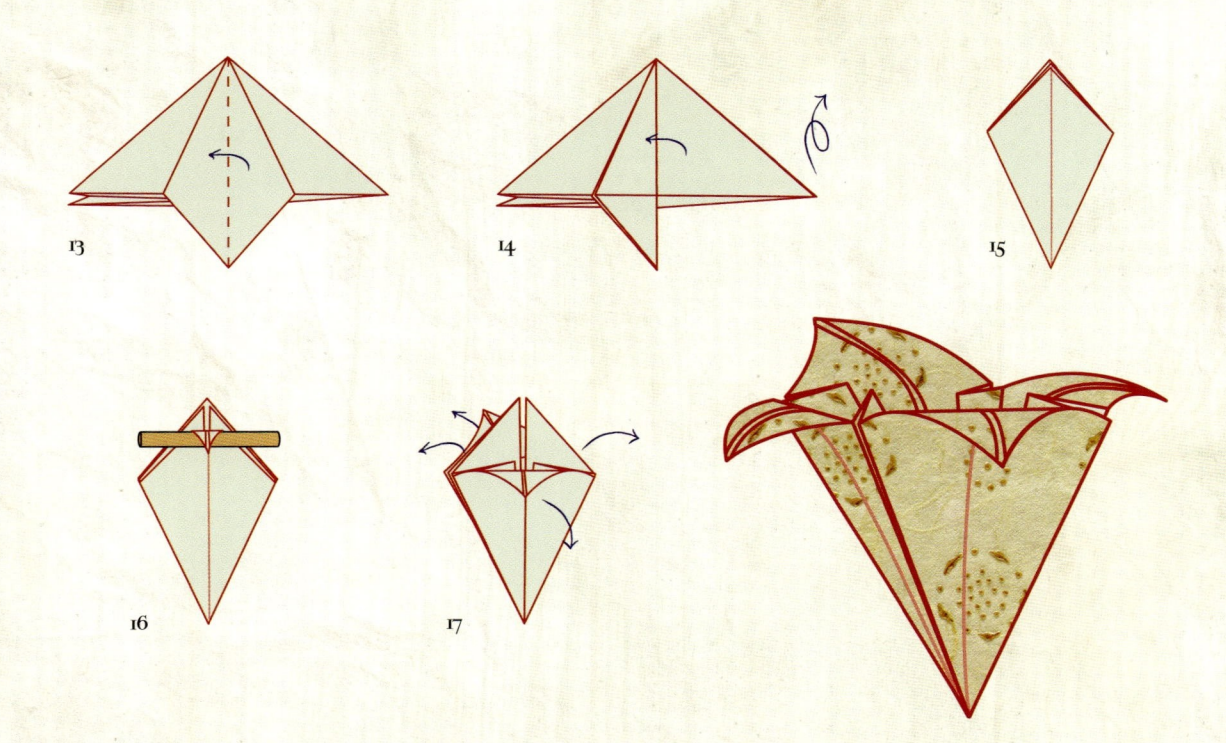

63

little butterflies

decorations for the home

cherry blossom branches

little butterflies

MATERIALS FOR TEN BUTTERFLIES
10 squares of patterned origami paper 7.5 x 7.5cm (2¾ x 2¾in) ♦ 10 squares of plain origami paper 7.5 x 7.5cm (2¾ x 2¾in) ♦ 10 hat pins ♦ 1 frame

EQUIPMENT
♦ 1 paper folder

folding

1. Line each square of patterned origami paper with a second square of plain, matching paper. Fold the centre lines then the diagonals along the dotted lines. Unfold.
2. Fold the whole square in half to the rear.
3. Lift the right-hand point vertically, opening it towards you. Open with the help of the scored creases.
4. Flatten and score the fold. Turn the left-hand point over towards the right along the dotted line.
5. Turn the left-hand point over again towards the right along the dotted line. Repeat steps 3 to 5.
6. Score the folds.
7. Fold in half so that the point is showing at the top. Turn the folding over.
8. Pull the first sheet open.
9. Open fully and crease so the piece lies flat against the work surface.
10. Score the folds in the square.
11. Change the position of the folds along the dotted lines. Score the new folds starting with the bottom points.
12. Cut along the centre fold, indicated in the diagram with a blue line, with a pair of scissors. Fold along the dotted lines.
13. Fold in half to the rear.
14. Fold along the dotted lines to give dimension to the body. Open.

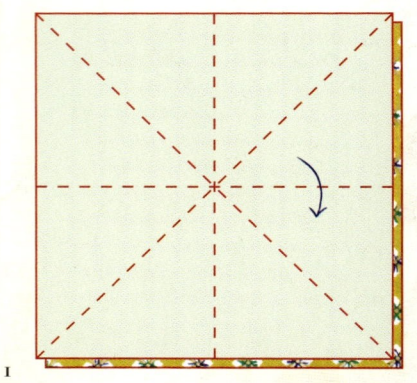

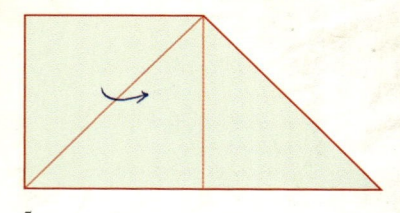

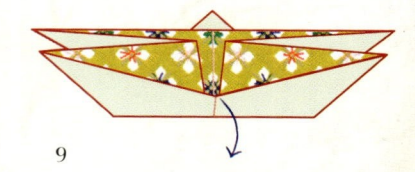

decorations for the home

difficulty 🌢🌢

assembly

Using hat pins, pin the butterflies into the frame in the desired positions.

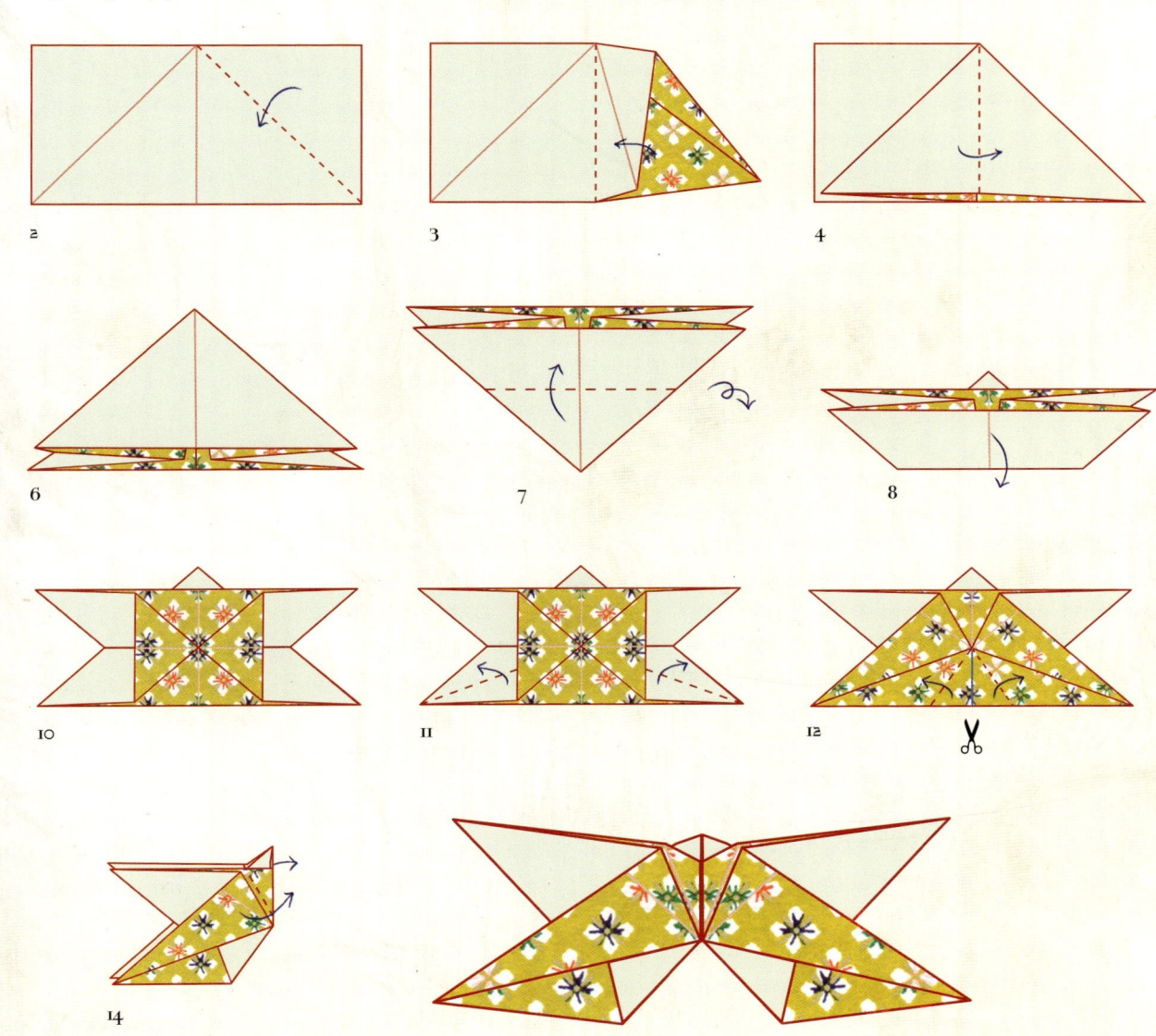

2

3

4

6

7

8

10

11

12

14

67

cherry blossom branches

MATERIALS FOR TWELVE FLOWERS
4 squares of plain pink and patterned pink origami paper 5 x 5cm (2 x 2in) ◆ 4 squares of the same paper 4 x 4cm (1½ x 1½in) ◆ 4 squares of the same paper 3 x 3cm (1¼ x 1¼in) ◆ scraps of pink origami paper ◆ 1 branch

EQUIPMENT
1 paper folder ◆ 1 tube of adhesive ◆ 1 pair of scissors ◆ 1 pencil

folding

1. Fold the square in half.
2. Score the fold along the dotted line, forming a crease.
3. Score the fold along the dotted line again, forming an opposing crease.
4. Fold along the dotted line so that the bottom left point matches the centre intersection of the previously scored folds.
5. Fold along the dotted line.
6. Fold along the dotted line again and score the top left corner as indicated.
7. Fold back one side to the rear, so the entire design is folded in half.
8. Draw the curve of the petal with a pencil and cut along the line.
9. Unfold the flower.
10. Fold one half-petal on to the facing one.
11. Do the same for each half-petal so that the flower is folded together.
12. Flatten the complete folding to form a single petal.
13. Fold along the dotted line and turn the folding over.
14. Fold along the dotted line.
15. Wrap over the bottom point of the flower. Open the flower and flatten keeping the folds on top of one another. Repeat for the remaining 11 flowers.

assembly

Choose a branch. Attach the flowers to the branch using a little piece of paper covered with adhesive.

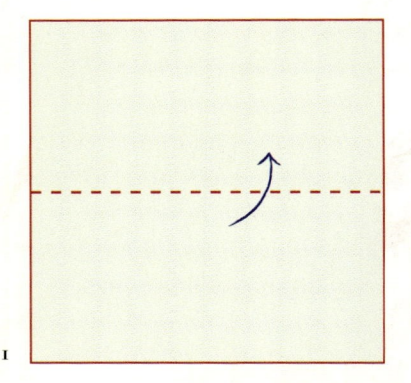

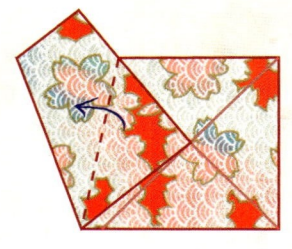

decorations for the home

difficulty ♦♦

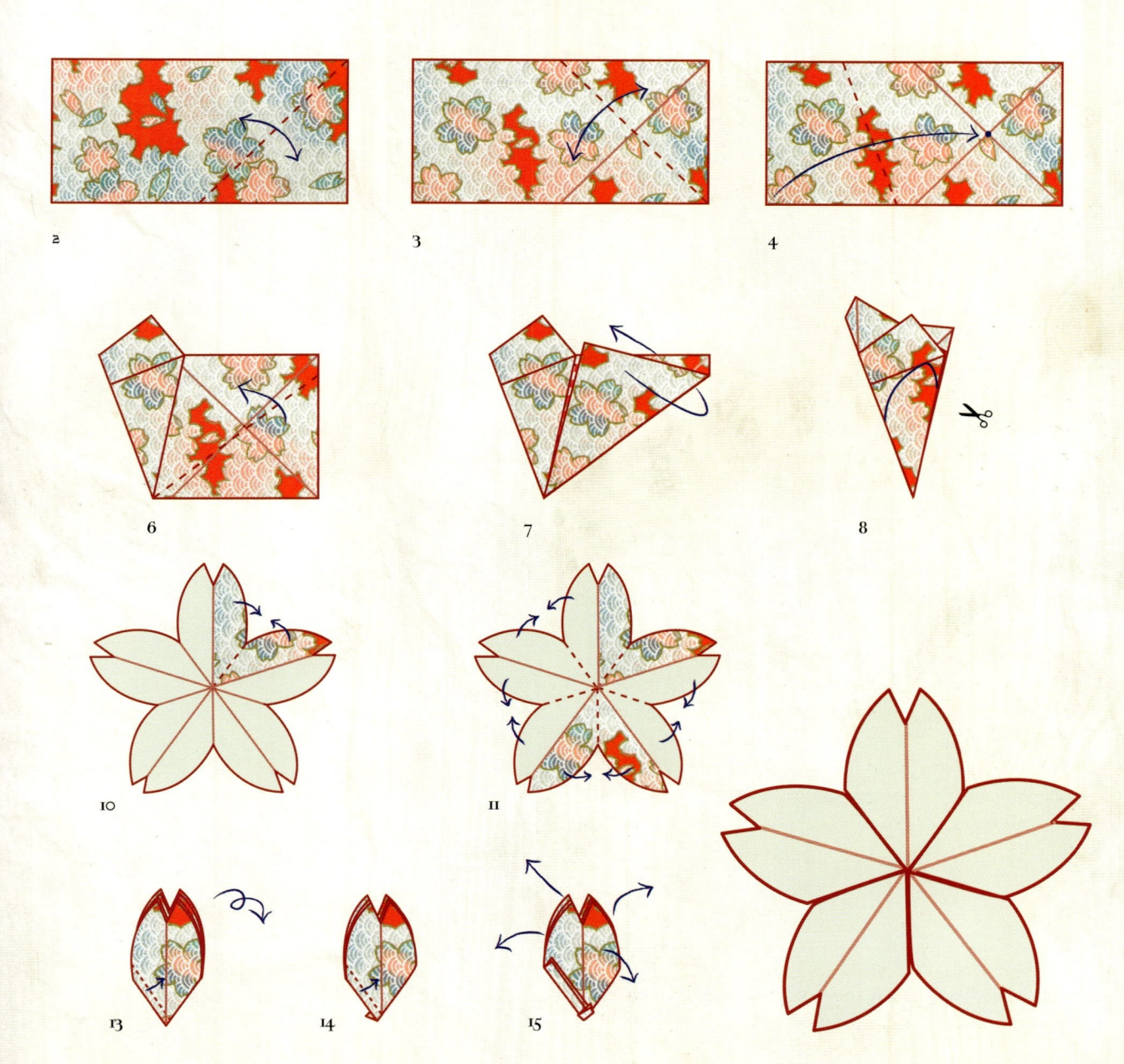

2

3

4

6

7

8

10

11

13

14

15

70

decorations for the home

pretty pendants

difficulty ◆

MATERIALS FOR ONE PENDANT
gold craft paper ◆ music score ◆ golden yellow sewing thread ◆ 1 sheet of tracing paper

EQUIPMENT
1 pencil ◆ 1 pair of scissors ◆ 1 tube of adhesive ◆ 1 sewing machine

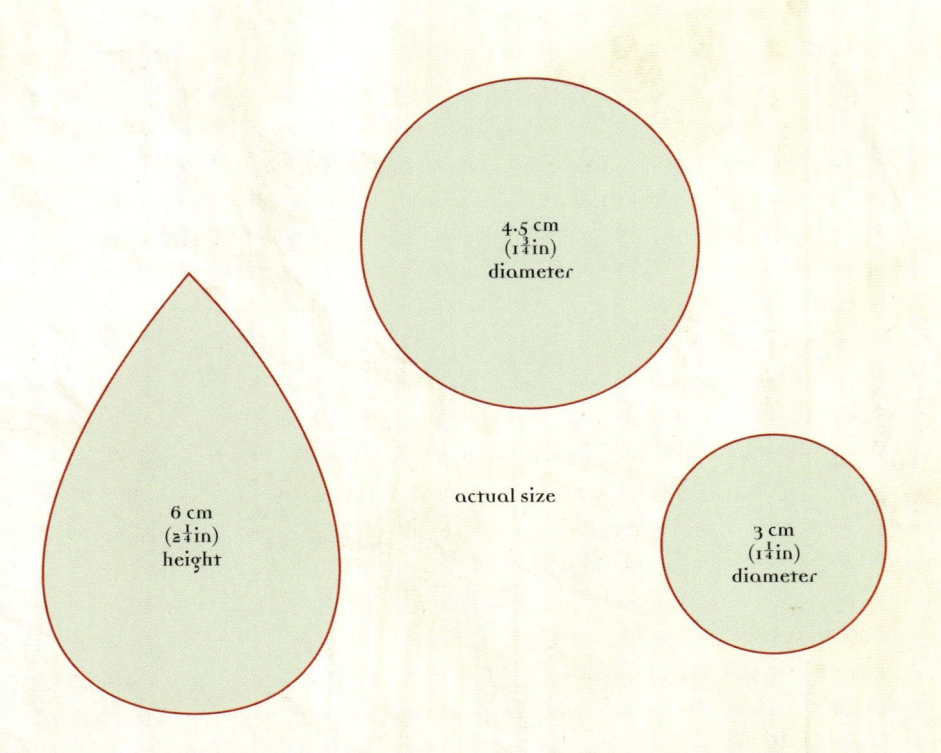

4.5 cm
($1\frac{3}{4}$in)
diameter

6 cm
($2\frac{1}{4}$in)
height

actual size

3 cm
($1\frac{1}{4}$in)
diameter

pretty pendants (cont.)

folding

1. Trace and transfer the drawing of the pendant twice on to the reverse of craft paper and music score. Cut out using a pair of scissors.
2. Fold each piece in half.
3. Taking the gold craft paper, glue the back of one half-fold to another from the music score.
4. Assemble the two half-pendants and glue together. Hold in place while the adhesive dries. Make as many pendants as required in the same way.
5. Repeat steps 1 to 4 with paper discs to make the balls.

assembly

Flatten each droplet/round pendant. Take a round pendant and, using the sewing machine, sew across the centre. Sew on the droplet pendant two centimetres (¾in) further along. Tie and trim the excess thread, leaving enough for hanging the pendant. Make a garland with the assembled discs in the same way as the pendants. Sew the balls by machine spacing them 1cm (½in) apart.

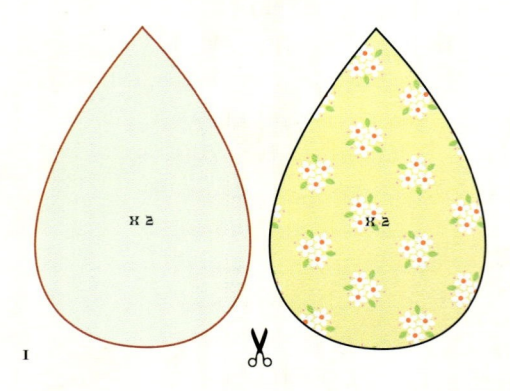

decorations for the home

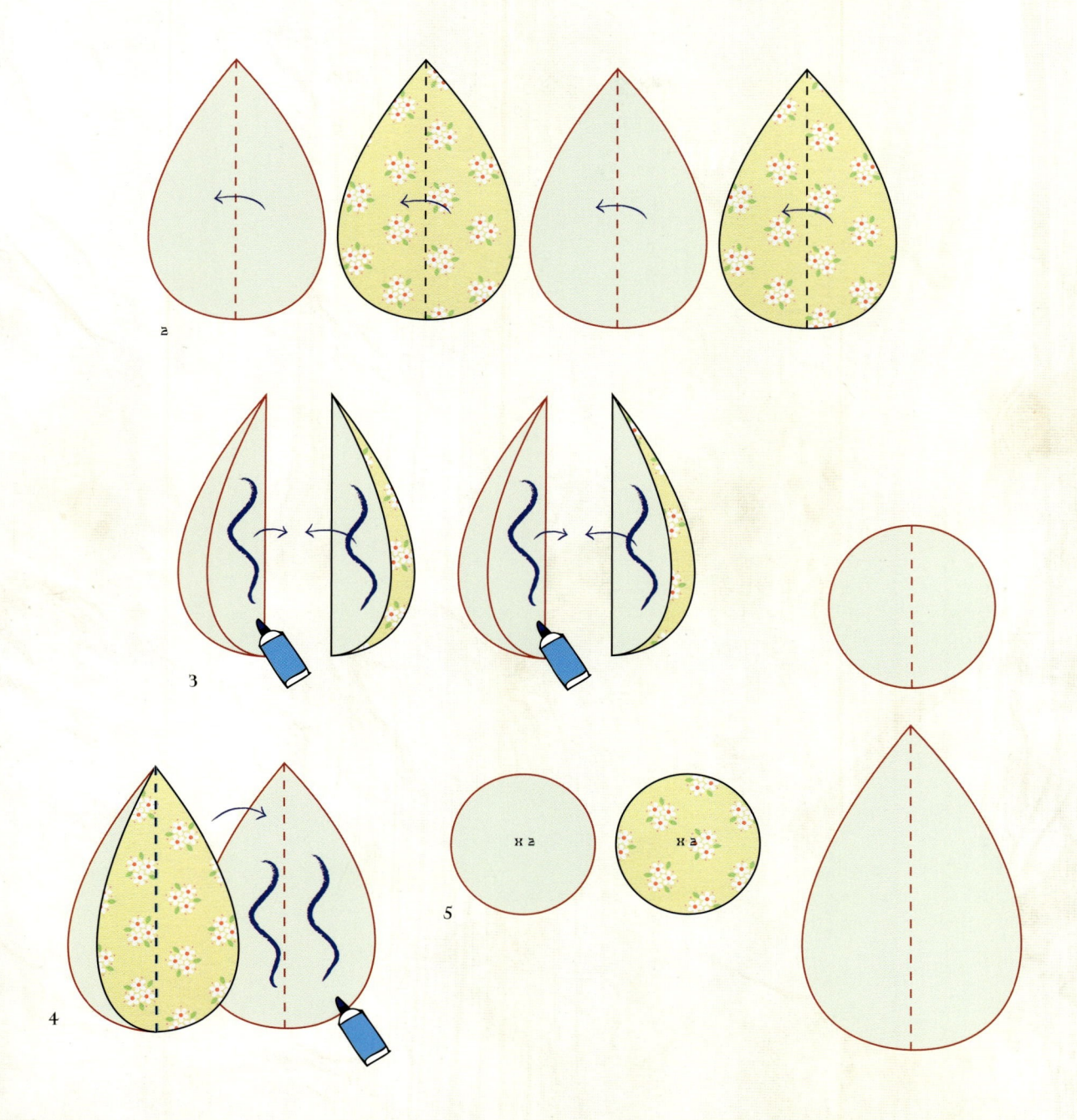

73

decorations for the home

paper lamp

difficulty ♦

MATERIALS FOR 1 LAMP
1 glass vase 28cm (11in) high and 10cm (4in) in diameter ♦ 1 rectangle of patterned origami paper 28 x 34cm (11 x 13½in) ♦ 1 disc of the same paper 10cm (4in) in diameter ♦ 1 strip of corrugated card 4 x 32cm (1½ x 12½in) long ♦ 1 card disc 10.3cm (4in) in diameter ♦ 1 strip of finely striped brown paper 4 x 32cm (1½ x 12½in) ♦ 1 string of LED electric light bulbs

EQUIPMENT
1 paper folder ♦ 1 pencil ♦ 1 pair of scissors ♦ 1 craft knife ♦ 1 cutting mat ♦ 1 ruler ♦ adhesive ♦ double-sided adhesive tape

assembly

Cut out a strip of patterned origami paper the same height as the vase. Place some double-sided adhesive tape on the outside of the vase at the top and bottom. Turn the vase upside down. Place the sheet of paper over the tape and wrap around the vase. Glue the overlap neatly with a line of adhesive. Attach the paper around the bottom rim of the vase with some adhesive tape. Attach the paper at the base of the vase with adhesive tape, turning the paper up into the interior. Draw and cut out a disc in matching origami paper 10cm (4in) in diameter. Attach to the top of the lamp using the double-sided adhesive tape.

Using the craft knife, cut out the card disc 10.3cm (4in) in diameter. Cut a small notch as shown, left. Cut a strip of corrugated card 4cm (1½in) wide and 32cm (12½in) long. Place the strip of corrugated card around the disc with the corrugated edge facing inwards. Attach with adhesive, stopping level with the notch. Hold firmly in place while the adhesive dries. Cover the card with a striped brown paper in the same size as the corrugated card. Stick down.

Fill the vase with a string of electric lights. Turn the vase over. Slip it into the cardboard base so that the wire for the lights fits through the notch.

N.B: As the vase is not fixed to the base, stand the lamp in a safe place.

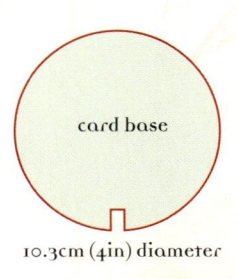

card base

10.3cm (4in) diameter

assembly

PARIS

SYDNEY

NEW YORK

SEOUL

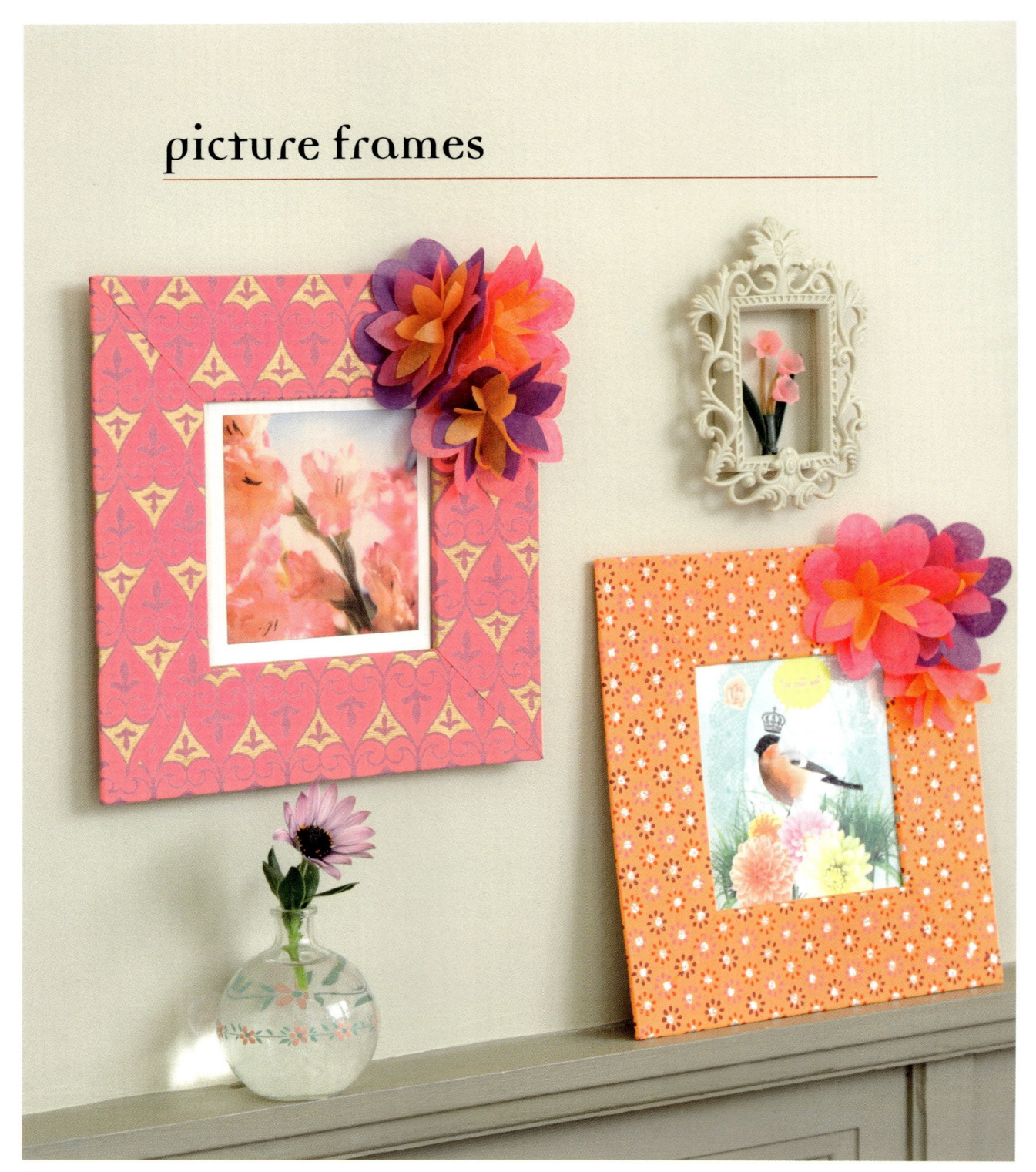

picture frames

hanging pendant

77

picture frames

MATERIALS FOR ONE FRAME

1 square of 1mm thick card 19 x 19cm (7½ x 7½in) ♦ 1 square of 1mm thick card 18 x 17cm (7 x 6¾in) ♦ 1 sheet of A4 Indian orange paper in floral pattern 21 x 29.7cm (8¼ x 11¾in) ♦ fuchsia pink silk paper ♦ orange silk paper ♦ violet silk paper ♦ 1 fixing for the frame

EQUIPMENT

1 pencil ♦ 1 craft knife ♦ 1 ruler ♦ 1 cutting mat ♦ white vinyl adhesive ♦ 1 paintbrush ♦ 1 pair of scissors

assembly

Measure and mark out the size of the front and the back of the frame on to card. Cut out with the craft knife and ruler on a cutting mat.

Measure and mark out the size of the Indian paper needed to cover the frame four times. Cut out with the craft knife and ruler in strips. Paint the reverse of the paper with white adhesive using the paintbrush. Attach to the front of the card. Smooth out to eliminate any bubbles. Turn the frame over. Apply adhesive over the excess paper, fold the edges over and press to the back.

Repeat the process until the whole frame is covered with the orange paper. Leave to dry under a press overnight.

The next day, spread adhesive on three sides of the back of the frame (be sure to leave one edge unglued). Glue it to the front of the frame and hold in place while the adhesive dries.

Fold each piece of silk paper into six (1), draw the shape of the petal and cut out using a pair of scissors (2). Make three flowers in the same way in different sizes and glue them to the frame.

Attach a fixing to the back of the frame.

decorations for the home

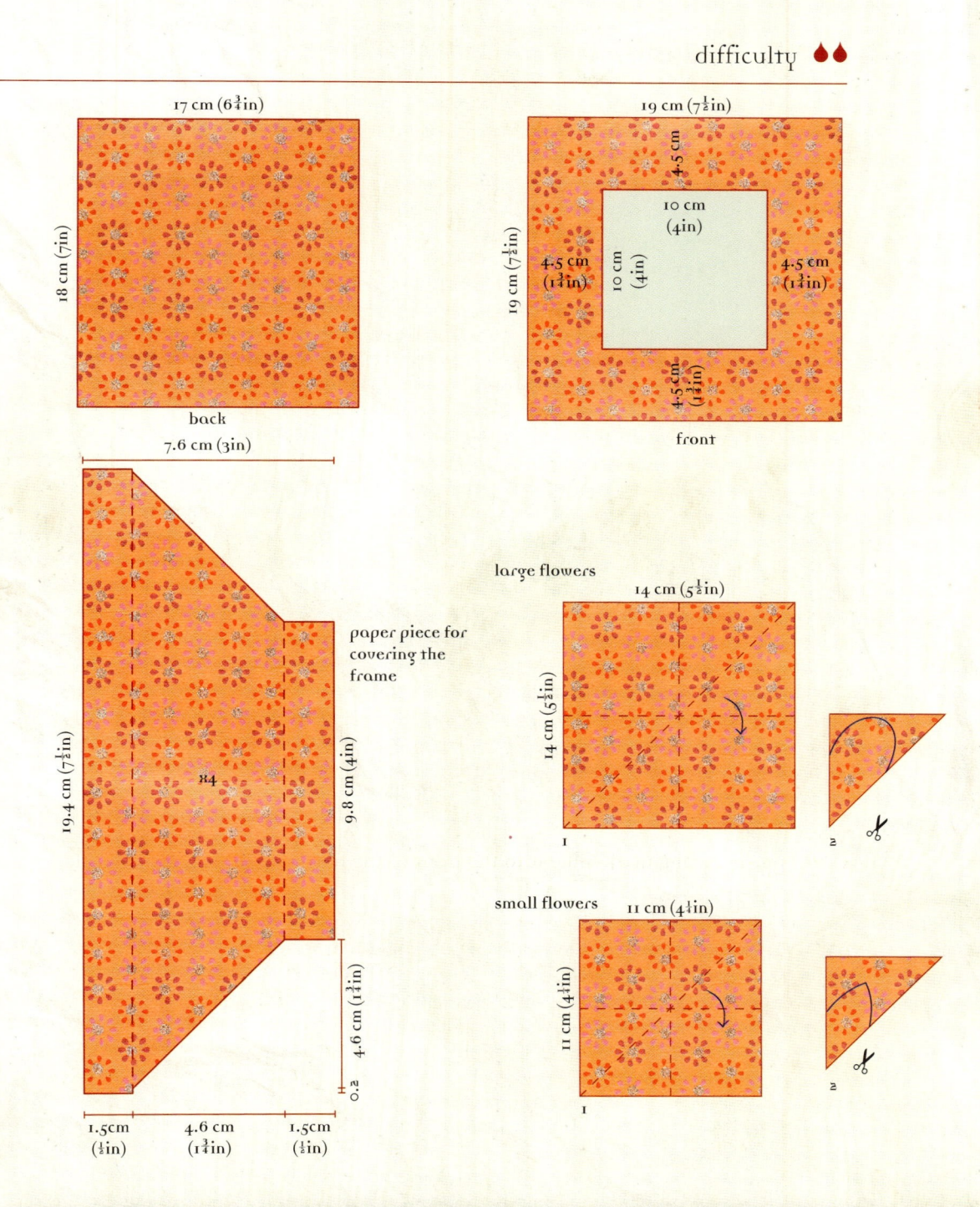

difficulty ♦♦

17 cm (6¾in)

18 cm (7in)

back

19 cm (7½in)

4.5 cm

10 cm (4in)

19 cm (7½in)

4.5 cm (1¾in)

10 cm (4in)

4.5 cm (1¾in)

4.5 cm (1¾in)

front

7.6 cm (3in)

paper piece for covering the frame

19.4 cm (7½in)

x4

9.8 cm (4in)

4.6 cm (1¾in)

0.2

1.5cm (½in) · 4.6 cm (1¾in) · 1.5cm (½in)

large flowers

14 cm (5½in)

14 cm (5½in)

1

2

small flowers

11 cm (4¼in)

11 cm (4¼in)

1

2

79

hanging pendant

MATERIALS FOR ONE HANGING DECORATION
1 strip of origami paper 0.5 x 30cm (¼ x 11¾in) ♦ 1 strip of golden origami paper 1 x 50cm (½ x 19¾in) ♦ twisted wire ♦ 1 large red bead ♦ crimp beads ♦ crystal beads ♦ yellow beads ♦ 1 earring finding with loop ♦ 1 decorative cone tip ♦ 1 crystal pendant

EQUIPMENT
1 pair of pliers ♦ 1 needle

folding

1. Make a flat knot at one end of the gold paper strip.
2. Thread the end and tighten the knot by gently tugging the long end to form a pentagon.
3. Turn the shortest end over towards the rear of the knot.
4. Fold the strip towards the rear along the dotted line.
5. Fold the strip towards the front to wrap it around the knot at the end, gently pulling it tight.
6. Fold to the rear and gently pull tight.
7. Continue folding until you reach the end of the strip, gently pulling tight each time the strip is pulled through.
8. Slide the end of the strip into the last fold to finish off.
9. Using your fingers, exert a slight pressure on all sides of the star to give it a puffed-up look.
10. Make the second star in the same way.

assembly

Gently pierce right through the middle of the stars from the bottom to the top using a sewing needle. Make the holes wide enough to thread wire through.

Thread one end of the twisted wire into the hole of the crystal pendant. Slide the two ends of wire into a crimp bead. Crimp using pliers firmly at the tip of the pendant. Trim the shortest end off. Add a cone tip. Hold in place with another crimp bead.

Place a crimp bead 1cm (½in) further along and crimp in place. Add a crystal bead, a yellow bead, a crystal bead and then another crimp bead.

decorations for the home

difficulty ♦♦

Attach a crimp bead approximately 1cm (½in) further along. Thread the little star on to the twisted wire.

One centimetre (½in) further along after the star, add a fifth crimp bead, a trio of crystal and yellow beads, then a crimp bead. Pinch the crimp beads.

Add two crimp beads on to the twisted wire, pass the end into the loop of an earring finding with loop and thread back through the two crimp beads. Pull tight. Pinch to crimp the beads. Thread the earring finding into the largest star. Make a loop using a pair of pliers. Thread the end of a new piece of twisted wire into this loop. Attach using a crimp bead.

Two centimetres (¾in) further on, attach a crimp bead, add a crystal bead, a large red bead, a crystal bead and a crimp bead. Another 1.5cm (½in) further on, add a crystal bead, a yellow bead then a crystal bead.

Slide on two crimp beads. Make a loop and pass the end of the wire back into the two crimp beads. Pinch firmly together. Trim off the excess wire.

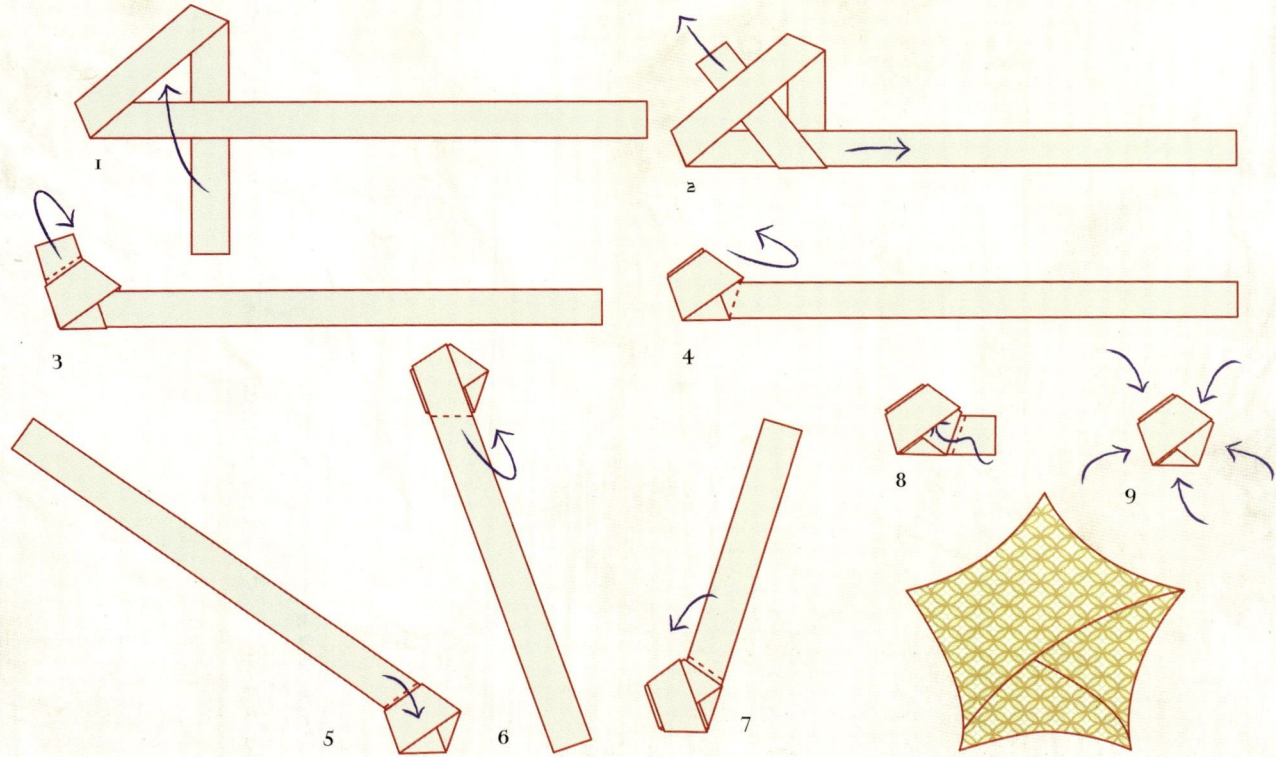

81

82

at the table

confectionery bags

at the table

water lily tea-light holders

confectionery bags

MATERIALS FOR ONE BAG

1 rectangle of coloured organza 10 x 20cm (4 x 7¾in) ♦ 1 rectangle of 210gsm (142lbs) thick paper in a matching colour 5 x 7.4cm (2 x 2¾in) ♦ 1 rectangle of 210gsm (142lbs) thick paper in a matching colour 2.2 x 7cm (¾ x 2¾in) ♦ 1 sheet of origami paper 12 x 12cm (4¾ x 4¾in) ♦ 1 scrap of plain paper ♦ 1 organza ribbon in a matching colour ♦ 1 brass fastener in the shape of a star ♦ 1 piece of copper wire

EQUIPMENT

1 pair of pliers ♦ 1 tapestry needle ♦ 1 pair of scissors ♦ 1 pencil ♦ 1 craft knife ♦ 1 cutting mat ♦ 1 ruler ♦ 1 sewing machine

folding

1. Cut 1 strip of organza 10 x 20cm (4 x 7¾in) long. Fold into three along the dotted lines.
2. Fold along the dotted line.
3. Fold over along the dotted line. Sew by machine.
4. Turn the design upside down so the opening is now at the base.
5. Press on the edges of the folding to give the triangular shape.
6. Cover a rectangle of thick paper 5 x 7.4cm (2 x 2¾in) with origami paper in a matching colour.
7. Place the rectangle, with patterned side facing down, on the table, and fold in half along the length. Unfold. Spread adhesive over the top edge of the paper as shown.
8. Attach this glued side to the outer edge of the bag. Place a rectangle of plain paper 2.2 x 7cm (¾ x 2¾in) on the edge of the bag. Hold in place while the adhesive dries.
9. Fold the flap and pierce a hole in the centre as shown.

templates:
organza

20 cm (7¾in)

flap

7.4cm (3in) — 5 cm (2in)

inside of the flap

7cm (2¾in) — 2.2 cm (¾in)

tag

4 cm (1½in) — 1.3 cm (½in)

flower
actual size

4 cm (1½in)

disc
actual size

1.3 cm (½in)

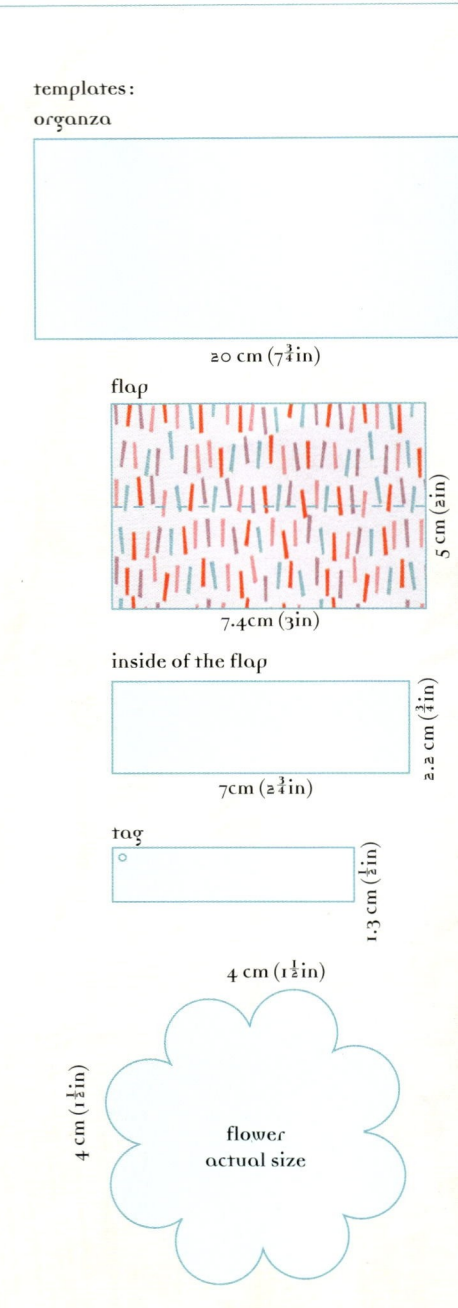

at the table

difficulty ♦♦

assembly

Trace the drawing of the flower. Transfer it to plain paper. Cut out with a pair of scissors. Pierce the centre of the flower.

Fill the bag with confectionery. Fold over the pierced flap to close the bag.

Cut off a piece of organza ribbon 10cm (4in) long. Make a loop. Position on the centre of the flap. Place the flower on top. Close by sliding a brass fastener in the shape of a star into the centre of the flower and through the flap.

Cut out a rectangular tag and cover with origami paper. Pierce a hole in it. Attach to the bag using a little piece of copper wire. Write on the name of the person that the bag is for. Place on the table.

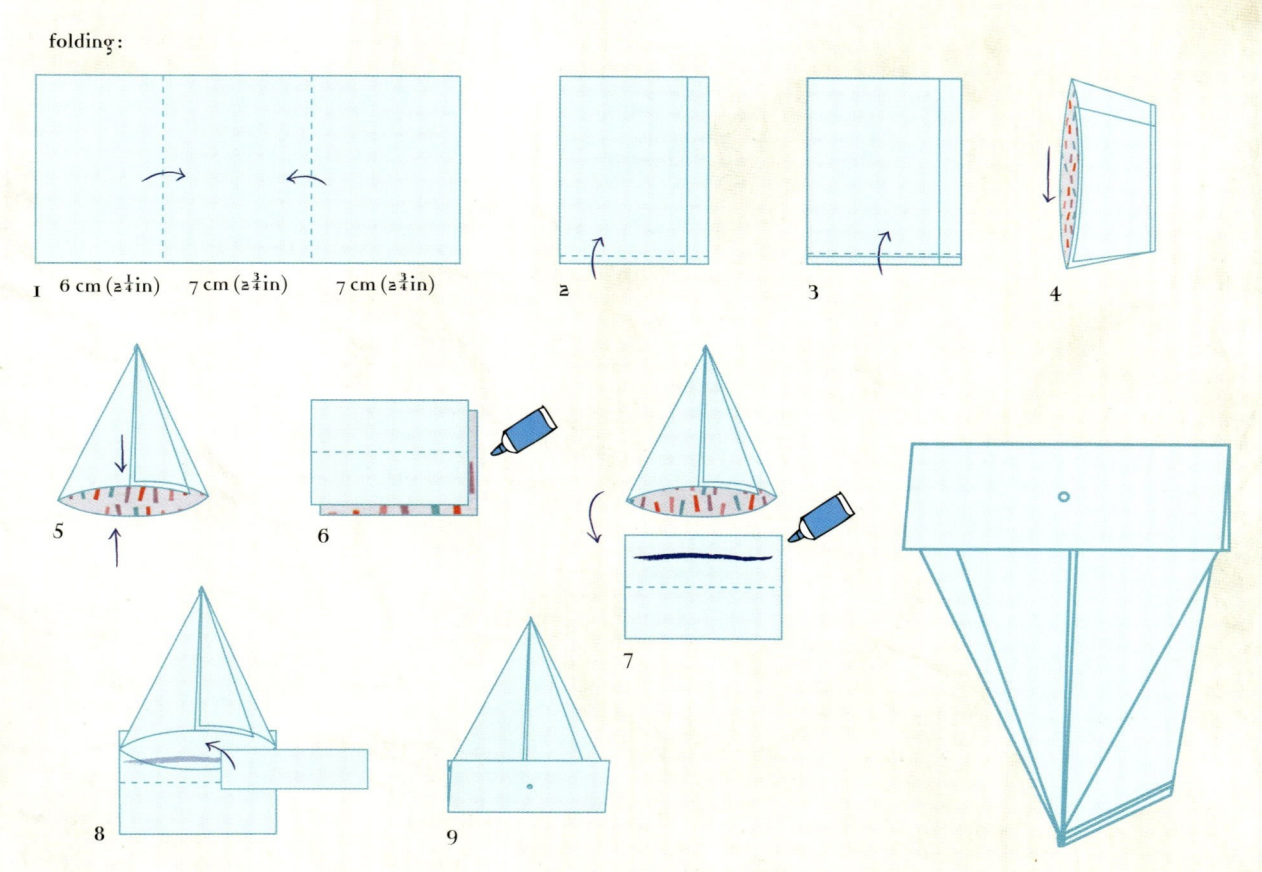

folding:

1 6 cm (2¼in)   7 cm (2¾in)   7 cm (2¾in)

water lily tea-light holders

MATERIALS FOR EIGHT LOTUS FLOWERS

3 squares of golden yellow, vanilla and light yellow mulberry paper 30 x 30cm (11¾ x 11¾in) ◊ 2 squares of the same paper 21 x 21cm (8¼ x 8¼in) ◊ 2 squares of the same paper 17 x 17cm (6¾ x 6¾in) ◊ 1 square of white mulberry paper 14 x 14cm (5½ x 5½in)

EQUIPMENT

1 paper folder ◊ 3 tea lights ◊ 3 glass tea light holders

folding

1. Fold along the centre lines. Score the folds with the paper folder. Unfold.
2. Fold along the dotted lines to fold the corners into the centre.
3. Fold along the dotted lines to fold the corners into the centre.
4. Fold along the dotted lines to fold the corners into the centre.
5. Turn the folding over with a quarter turn.

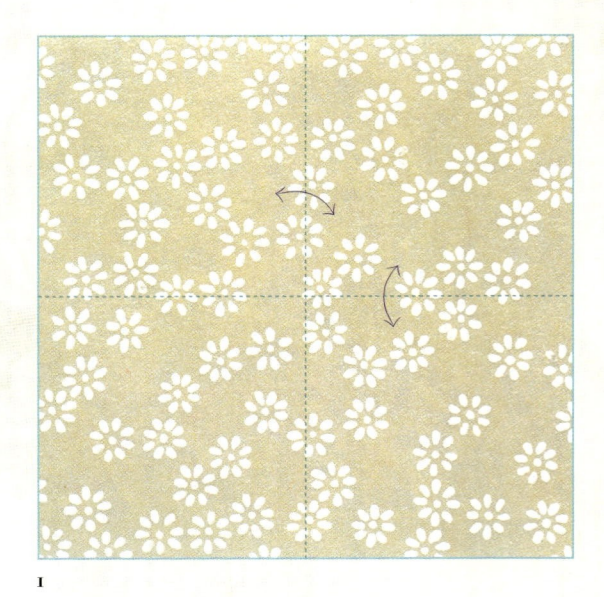

at the table

difficulty 🌢🌢

6. Fold along the dotted line to fold the corners into the centre.
7. Fold along the dotted lines to fold over the points.
8. Turn the folding over.
9. Pick up one point from the centre. Gently pull towards the rear to make the first petal. Repeat the process with the three other points.
10. Repeat step 9 with the points at the centre.
11. Fold along the dotted lines. Turn the folding over.

Place a glass tea-light holder in the centre of the largest lotus flowers and insert a tea light.

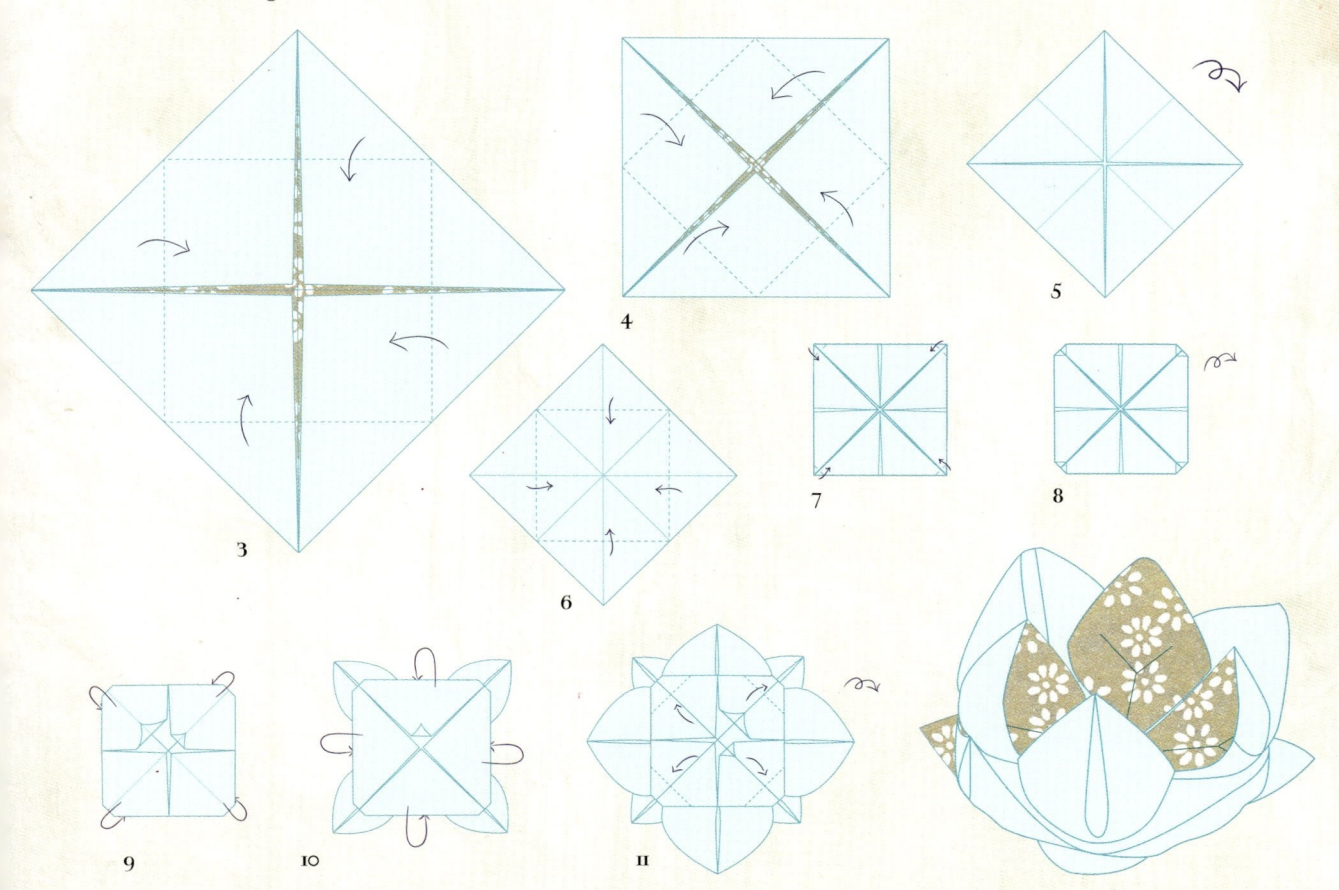

89

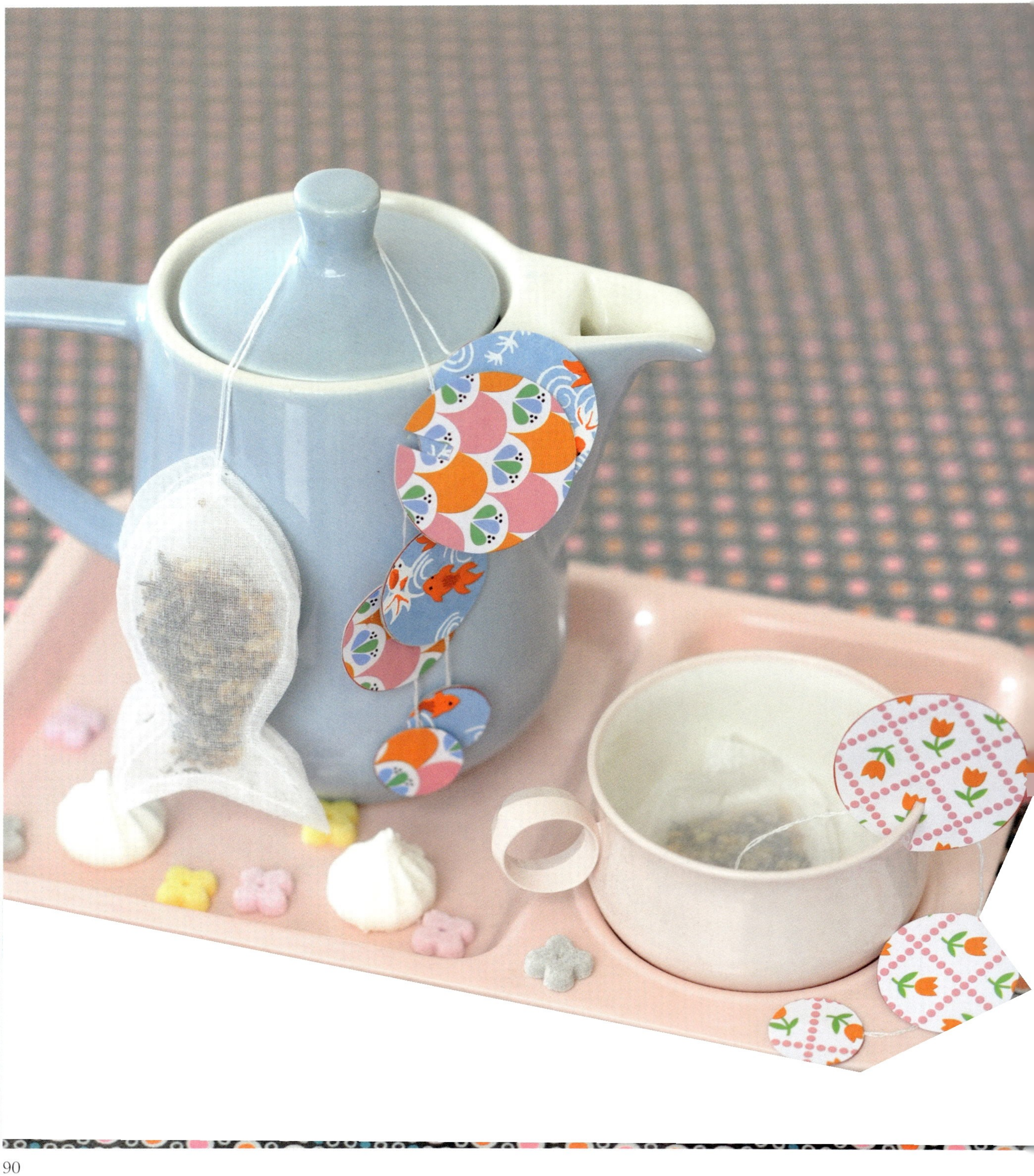

at the table

fish are my cup of tea

difficulty ♦

MATERIALS FOR 5 FISH
1 piece of white organza 10 x 21cm (4 x 8¼in) ♦ 1 sheet of patterned origami paper 15 x 15cm (6 x 6in) ♦ white cotton thread

EQUIPMENT
1 pair of scissors ♦ 1 pencil ♦ 1 compass ♦ 1 piece of tailor's chalk ♦ 1 sewing machine

assembly

Trace the fish motif below on to a sheet of white paper and cut it out. This will serve as a template. Pin the template of the fish to the fabric. Draw around it with the tailor's chalk. Cut out two fish using a pair of scissors.

Tie a knot in one end of a piece of cotton thread. Slide the thread between two fish at the mouth. Machine sew starting at the tail of the fish and leave an opening.

Fill the bag with tea of your choice. Close up with the sewing machine. Draw three pairs of circles using the compass on the reverse of a sheet of origami paper using the diagrams below. Cut a notch on the two larger discs as shown. Align the cotton thread, which is attached to the the fish, on the insides of these discs. Two centimetres (¾in) further along, glue on the two medium-sized discs. Finish by glueing the smallest discs to the thread.

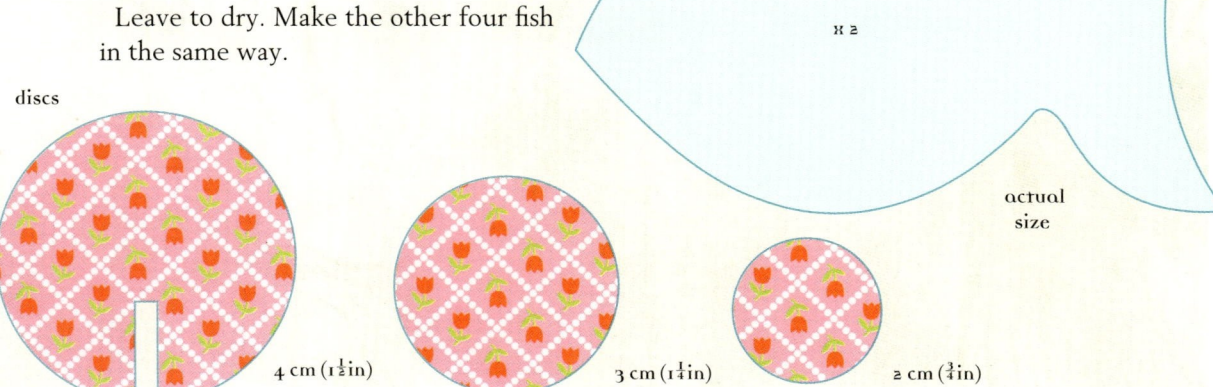

Leave to dry. Make the other four fish in the same way.

fish / tea bag

x 2

actual size

discs

4 cm (1½in)   3 cm (1¼in)   2 cm (¾in)

at the table

little tea caddies

difficulty ◆

MATERIALS FOR ONE CADDY
sheet of origami paper 21 x 29.7cm (8¼ x 11¾in) ◆ 1 metal tea caddy

EQUIPMENT
1 pencil ◆ 1 ruler ◆ 1 craft knife ◆ 1 cutting mat ◆ vinyl adhesive ◆ 1 paintbrush ◆ 1 pair of scissors ◆ 1 compass

assembly

Measure the height and circumference of the tea caddy without its lid. Transfer the measurements to the reverse of the origami paper and cut it out. Paint adhesive on the reverse of the paper using a paintbrush. Apply the paper to the caddy and smooth out to remove any bubbles. Leave to dry.

Transfer the dimensions for the height of the lid to the back of the origami paper and add 1.5cm (½in). Paint adhesive on the reverse of the paper, using a paintbrush. Apply to the edge of the lid and smooth out to remove any bubbles. Cut slits and fold the excess paper down over the lid.

Measure the diameter of the lid. Transfer the measurements to the reverse of some origami paper. Draw a circle using a compass, following these measurements. Paint glue on to the reverse of the paper disc using a paintbrush.

Apply the paper to the lid. Smooth out with your hand to remove any bubbles. Leave to dry.

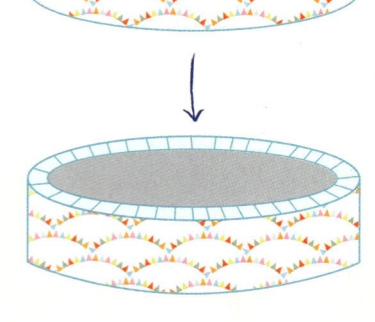

93

94

at the table

cake doilies

difficulty ◆

MATERIALS FOR 3 DOILIES
3 squares of origami paper 10 x 10cm (4 x 4in) ◆ 3 squares of tracing paper in matching colours 10 x 10cm (4 x 4in) ◆ sewing thread in matching colours ◆ 1 sheet of ordinary tracing paper

EQUIPMENT
1 pair of scissors ◆ 1 pencil ◆ 1 craft knife ◆ 1 ruler ◆ 1 cutting mat ◆ 1 sewing machine

assembly

Trace the flower motif. Transfer to the reverse of a sheet of origami paper. Cut out. Fold along the dotted lines. Take a piece of coloured tracing paper. Place on the drawing of the star. Trace. Cut out with the craft knife and ruler. Fold the star along the dotted lines to mark the centre of each branch.

Place the star in the middle of the flower. Hold firmly in place and sew by machine along the creases scored. Tie off the excess threads and cut.

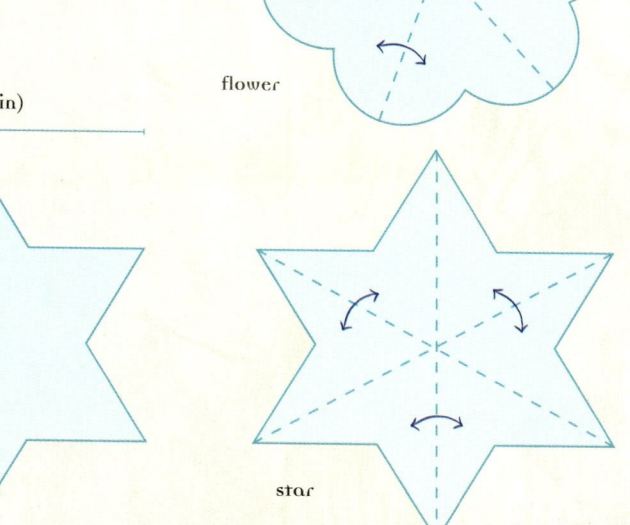

flower

8.8 cm (3½in)

star

at the table

party parasols and decorations

difficulty ◆

MATERIALS FOR THREE PARASOLS
3 squares of origami paper 10 x 10cm (4 x 4in) ◆ 3 squares of paper in matching colours 10 x 10cm (4 x 4in) ◆ 3 skewers ◆ cocktail sticks ◆ pink paint ◆ blue paint

EQUIPMENT
1 pair of scissors ◆ 1 pencil ◆ 1 paintbrush ◆ 1 compass ◆ 1 tube of adhesive ◆ 1 embroidery needle

folding

Parasols: On the reverse of a sheet of origami paper, draw a circle for the parasol using a compass. Cut out using a pair of scissors and cut across the radius to the centre. Place one edge over the other to form a cone. Apply a line of adhesive between the two edges of the paper. Hold in place while the adhesive dries.

Trace the drawing for the border. Transfer to a piece of plain paper. Cut out using a pair of scissors. Glue beneath the parasol and pierce the centre with the needle.

Cut a piece of skewer 10cm (4in) long. Paint it blue. Leave to dry. Slide into the centre of the parasol.

Make several parasols in the same way.

Flags: Trace the flag of template. Transfer to the reverse of a sheet of patterned origami paper. Cut out. Score the fold. Apply a line of adhesive. Place a cocktail stick in the fold. Hold in place while the adhesive dries. Make several flags in the same way.

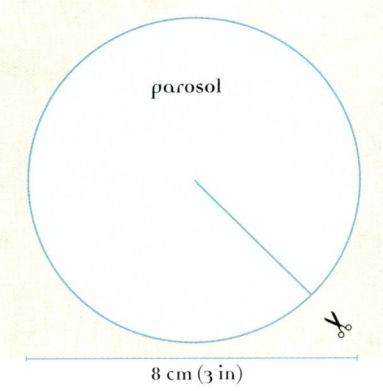

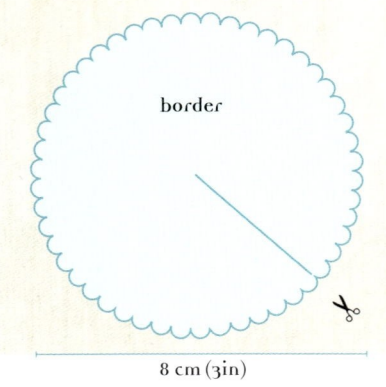

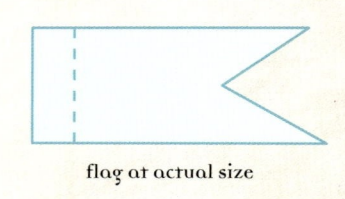

parasol

border

flag at actual size

8 cm (3 in)

8 cm (3in)

97

98

celebrations

celebrations

advent stockings

difficulty ♦♦

MATERIALS FOR ONE ADVENT CALENDAR
red craft paper ♦ gold craft paper ♦ beige Indian paper with gold patterns ♦ red Indian paper with gold patterns ♦ 1 sheet of beige paper ♦ small stockings: 11.5 x 14cm (4¼ x 5½in) ♦ medium stockings: 14 x 14cm (5½ x 5½in) ♦ large stockings: 14 x 17cm (5½ x 6¾in) ♦ the top lining: 1.5 x 14cm (½ x 5½in) ♦ red cotton thread ♦ white cotton thread ♦ metallic gold thread

EQUIPMENT
1 paper folder ♦ 1 embroidery needle ♦ 1 pair of scissors ♦ 1 pencil ♦ 1 craft knife ♦ 1 cutting mat ♦ 1 ruler ♦ 1 tube of adhesive

folding

1. Select a type of paper and cut to size. Fold along the central dotted lines Unfold.
2. Fold over along the dotted lines.
3. Fold along the dotted line.
4-5. Score the fold with the paper folder along the dotted lines and open.

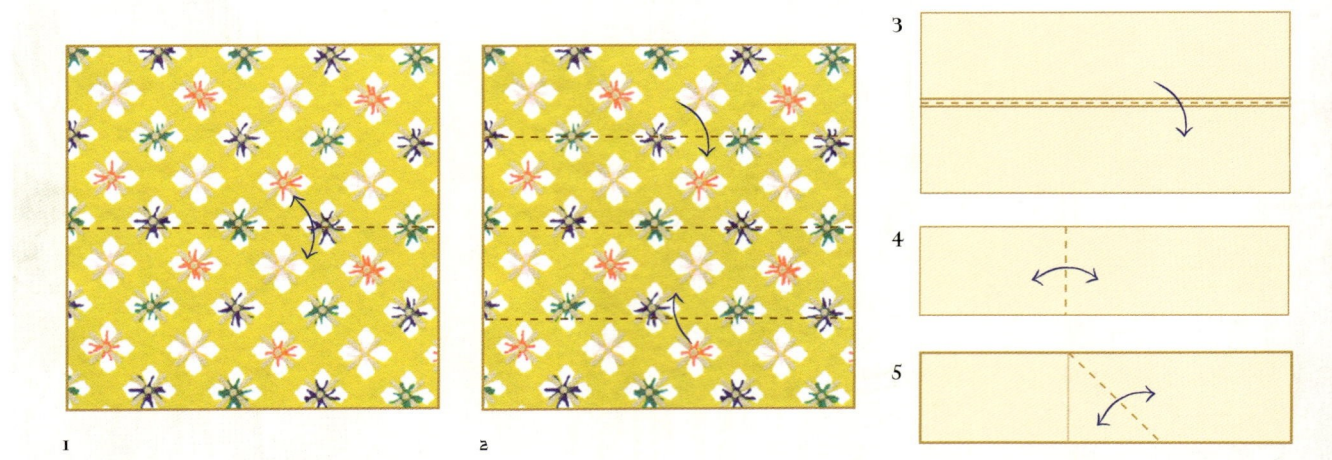

101

advent stockings (cont.)

6. Open the right-hand part of the folding and fold along the dotted line.
7. Flatten the folding. Fold along the dotted line.
8. Fold along the dotted line.
9. Score the fold along the dotted line.
10. Invert the fold inside the stocking. Fold over the two points of the stocking along the dotted lines.
11. Glue the end of the stocking closed. Hold in place while the adhesive dries.
12. Pivot the folding by a quarter turn in the direction of the arrows.
13. Open the top of the stocking.
14. Unfold the right-hand part of the stocking completely. Cut along the blue line. Unfold the top right corner as shown.
15. Fold over the top right corner along the dotted line as shown.
16. Slide the right sheet under the left sheet.
17. Apply a line of adhesive and fold over the left-hand part. Hold in place while the adhesive dries.
18. Pivot the folding in the direction of the arrows.
19. Cut out the turn-down for the stocking in a different paper. Glue to the top of the stocking. Fold around and hold in place while the adhesive dries.
20. Cut out the discs 1.5cm (½in) in diameter. Write a number on each one and glue them to the front of the stockings.

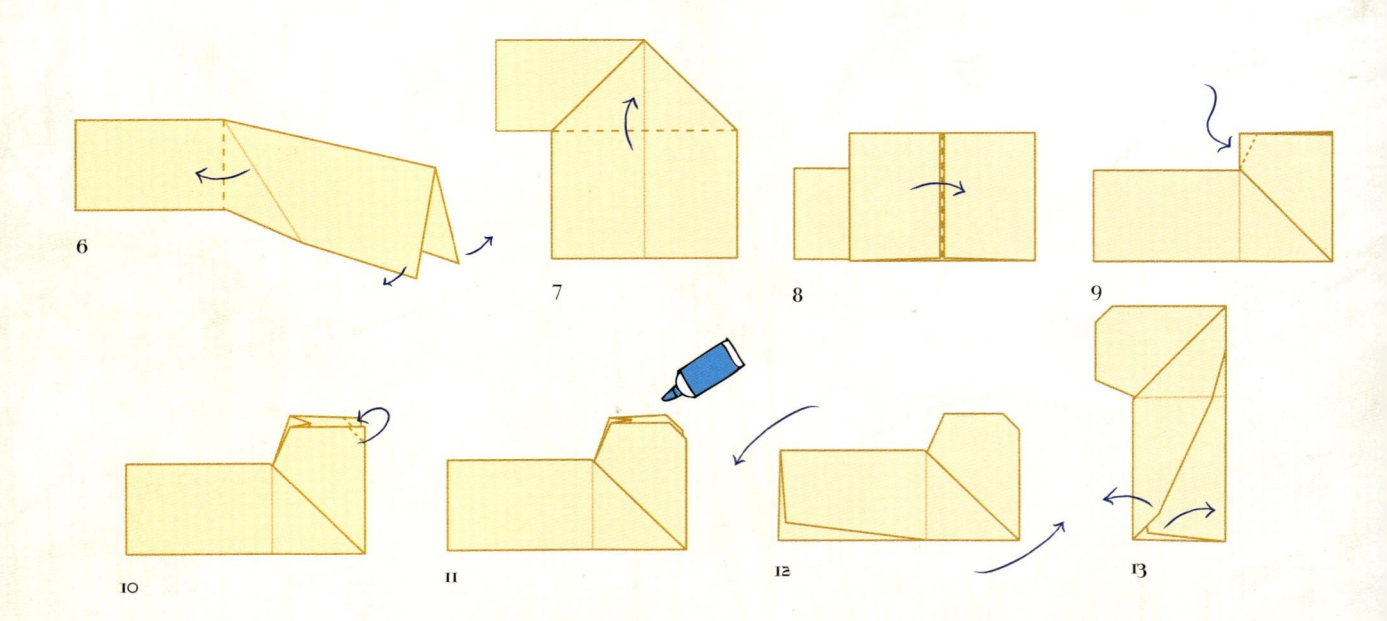

celebrations

14 15 16

17 18

19 20

assembly

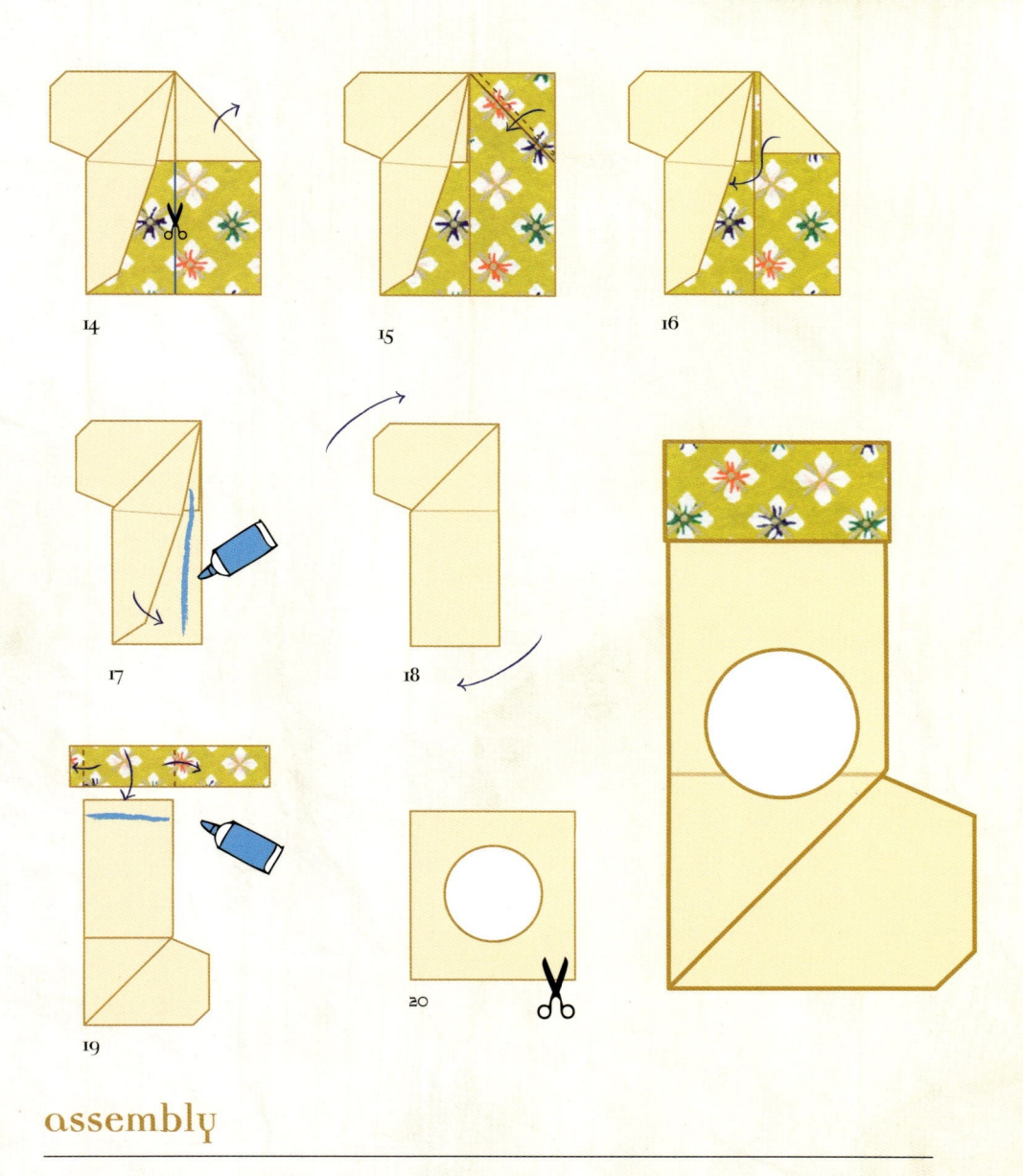

Make the 24 Christmas stockings in different coloured papers in varying heights, following the folding instructions. Decorate them with red, white or gold thread.

103

celebrations

gift boxes

difficulty ♦♦

MATERIALS FOR 3 BOXES AND EMBELLISHMENTS
1 square of 170g (6oz) red paper 9.5 x 9.5cm (3¾ x 3¾in) ♦ 1 square of 120g (4oz) red paper 11 x 11cm (4¼ x 4¼in) ♦ 1 square of 120g red paper 14 x 14cm (4¼ x 4¼in) ♦ red cotton thread ♦ scrap of red paper

MATERIALS FOR LIDS
1 square of red and white gift paper 10 x 10cm (4 x 4in) ♦ 1 square of 170g (6oz) white paper 10 x 10cm (4 x 4in) ♦ 1 square of red and white gift paper 12 x 12cm (4¾ x 4¾in) ♦ 1 square of white paper 12 x 12cm (4¾ x 4¾in) ♦ 1 square of red and white gift paper 15 x 15cm (6 x 6in) ♦ 1 square of white paper 15 x 15cm (6 x 6in)

EQUIPMENT
1 paper folder ♦ 1 compass ♦ 1 pair of scissors ♦ 1 pencil ♦ 1 tapestry needle ♦ 1 tube of adhesive

folding

1. To make a box, take a square of red paper and mark the centre of the diagonals with a pencil. (To make the lids, first line the gift paper with white paper.)
2. Fold the points over to the centre. Score the folds with a paper folder.

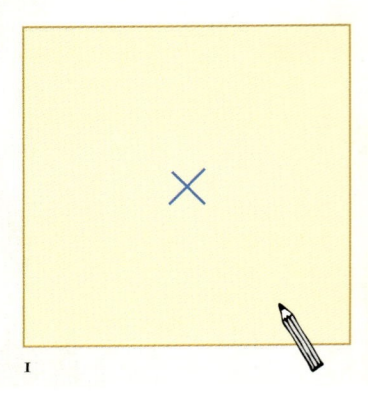

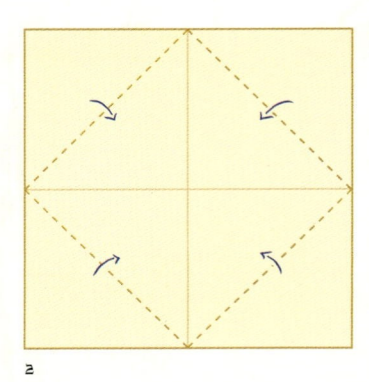

105

gift boxes (cont.)

3. Pivot the folding by a quarter turn.
4. Fold along the dotted lines. Flatten the folds with the paper folder. Unfold.
5. Fold along the dotted lines. Flatten the folds with the paper folder. Unfold.
6. Open the two opposite points and flatten.
7. Cut four slits along the blue lines using a pair of scissors.
8. Fold along the dotted lines.
9. Assemble the box by joining together the opposite points, indicated by the arrows.
10. Fold the top of the sheet over to the centre of the box. Fold over the two points at the sides, one against the other to make the last side of the box.
11. Fold over the last point to the centre of the box. Hold the points in place at the centre with a spot of adhesive.

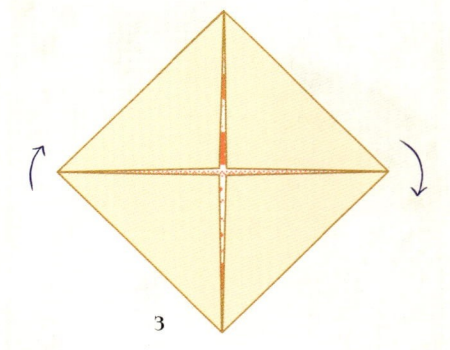

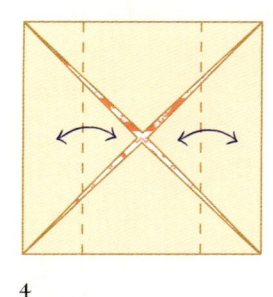

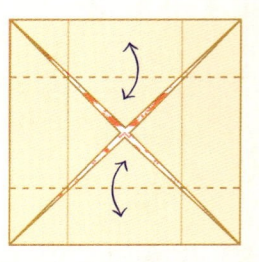

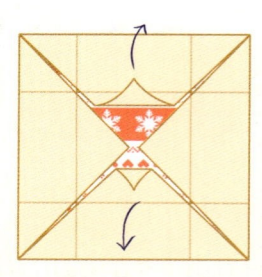

celebrations

7 8 9

10 11

assembly

After assembling the boxes and their lids, make the labels by using a compass to draw a disc 5cm (2in) in diameter on a scrap sheet of red paper. Pierce a hole in it using a tapestry needle.

Place a gift inside the box and attach its lid. Decorate by tying some red cotton thread around it. Slip one end of the thread through the hole in the label and write the recipient's name on it.

108

celebrations

happy new year card

difficulty ◆

MATERIALS FOR ONE CARD
1 square of origami paper 15 x 15cm (6 x 6in) ◆ 1 card 13.5 x 13.5cm (5¼ x 5¼in) (when folded) ◆ 1 envelope 14 x 14cm (5½ x 5½in) ◆ scrap of origami paper

EQUIPMENT
1 paper folder ◆ 1 flower-shaped hole punch (optional) ◆ 1 tube of adhesive

folding

Follow the folding instructions on pages 15–17 to make the crane.

assembly

Cover the card with a sheet of origami paper. Glue the back of the crane to the centre of the card. Cut out some flowers using the hole punch (or use the templates below) from the same paper as the crane. Glue to the card.

flowers at actual size

celebrations

christmas decorations

difficulty ♦♦

MATERIALS FOR FIVE DECORATIONS
6 squares of red patterned Indian paper 10 x 10cm (4 x 4in) ♦ 4 squares of beige patterned Indian paper 10 x 10cm (4 x 4in) ♦ 2 strips of red-patterned Indian paper 1 x 30cm (½ x 11¾in) ♦ 3 strips of beige patterned Indian paper 1 x 30cm (½ x 11¾in) ♦ red beads ♦ gold beads ♦ DMC gold metal effect stranded cotton thread

EQUIPMENT
1 paper folder ♦ 1 embroidery needle ♦ 1 pair of scissors ♦ 1 pencil ♦ 1 craft knife ♦ 1 cutting mat ♦ 1 ruler

folding

1. Score the centre folds and the diagonals. Fold to the rear along a diagonal line as shown below.
2. Score the fold along the dotted line. Unfold.
3. Lift the top point towards you.

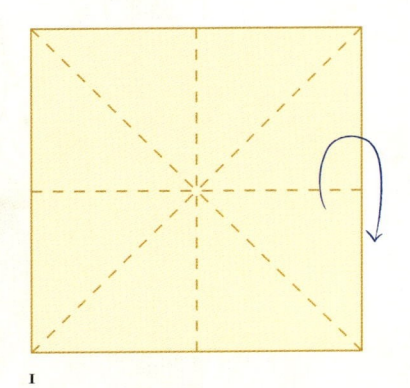

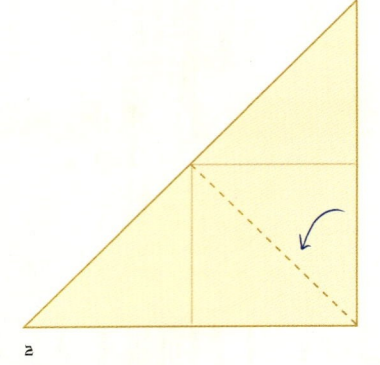

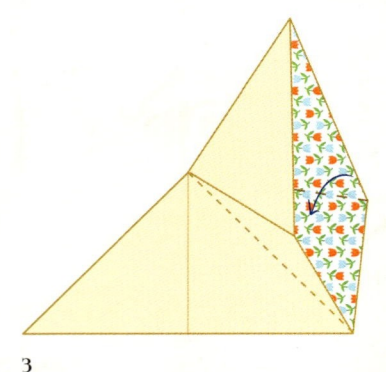

111

christmas decorations (cont.)

4. Open with the help of the scored creases.
5. Flatten and score the folds. Turn the folding over.
6. Repeat steps 3 to 5 with the point just formed. Flatten the folds.
7. Pivot the folding by a quarter turn.
8. Fold the top sheets along the dotted lines.
9. Turn the folding over.
10. Fold along the dotted lines.
11. Flatten the folding.
12. Take the bottom point and fold along the dotted line.
13. Score the fold. Turn the folding over.
14. Repeat steps 12 to 13. Assemble the folding along the dotted lines.
15. Make the second part of the decoration by repeating steps 1 to 14 with a second sheet of paper.
16. Using the strips of Indian paper, make 3 beige stars and 2 red stars following the folding instructions on pages 80–81.
17. To make the pendant for decoration, thread an embroidery needle with a piece of gold metallic thread and tie a knot at one end. Slide this inside the folding, bringing it out through the top point. Slide on a coloured bead. Tie another knot 2cm (¾in) above this point, add an alternately coloured bead and tie a third knot. Thread on an origami star. Add a another bead and secure with a final knot.
18. Fit the two foldings one inside the other. Slide the point of the first folding into the turned back corner of the second. Fit the four sides of the foldings together at the same time.
19. Make a loop with the thread to hang the decoration. Repeat the whole process for the four remaining stars.

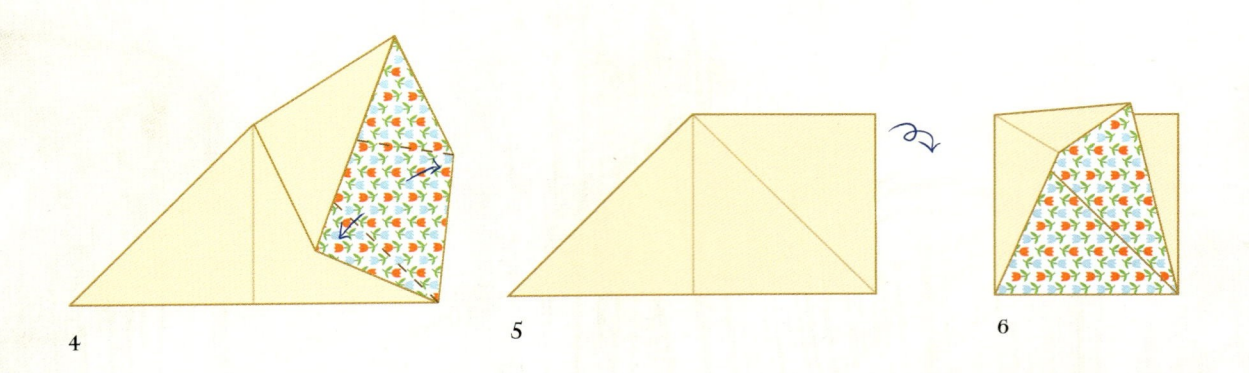

4   5   6

celebrations

7 8 9

10 11 12 13

14 15 16 17

18

19

113

114

celebrations

sweetie bags

difficulty ♦♦

MATERIALS FOR ONE BAG
1 square of origami paper 20 x 20cm (7¾ x 7¾in) ♦ 1 strip of matching plain paper ♦ 2 white cords 16cm (6¼in)

EQUIPMENT
1 paper folder ♦ 1 embroidery needle ♦ 1 pair of scissors ♦ 1 pencil ♦ 1 love heart hole punch ♦ 1 tube of adhesive

folding

1. Fold the centre lines, and then the diagonals along the dotted lines. Unfold.
2. Fold the square in half vertically, then fold along the dotted line as shown.

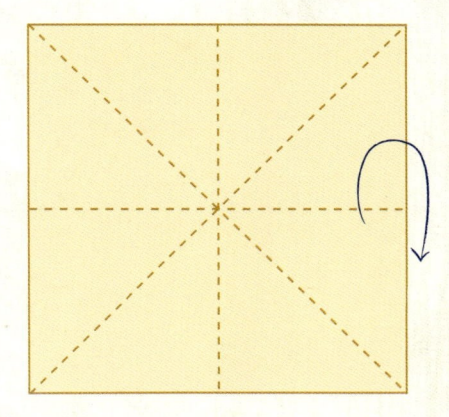

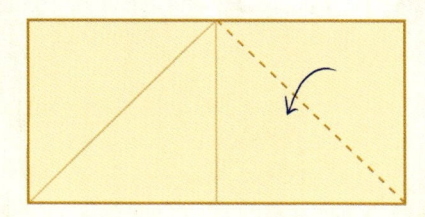

sweetie bags (cont.)

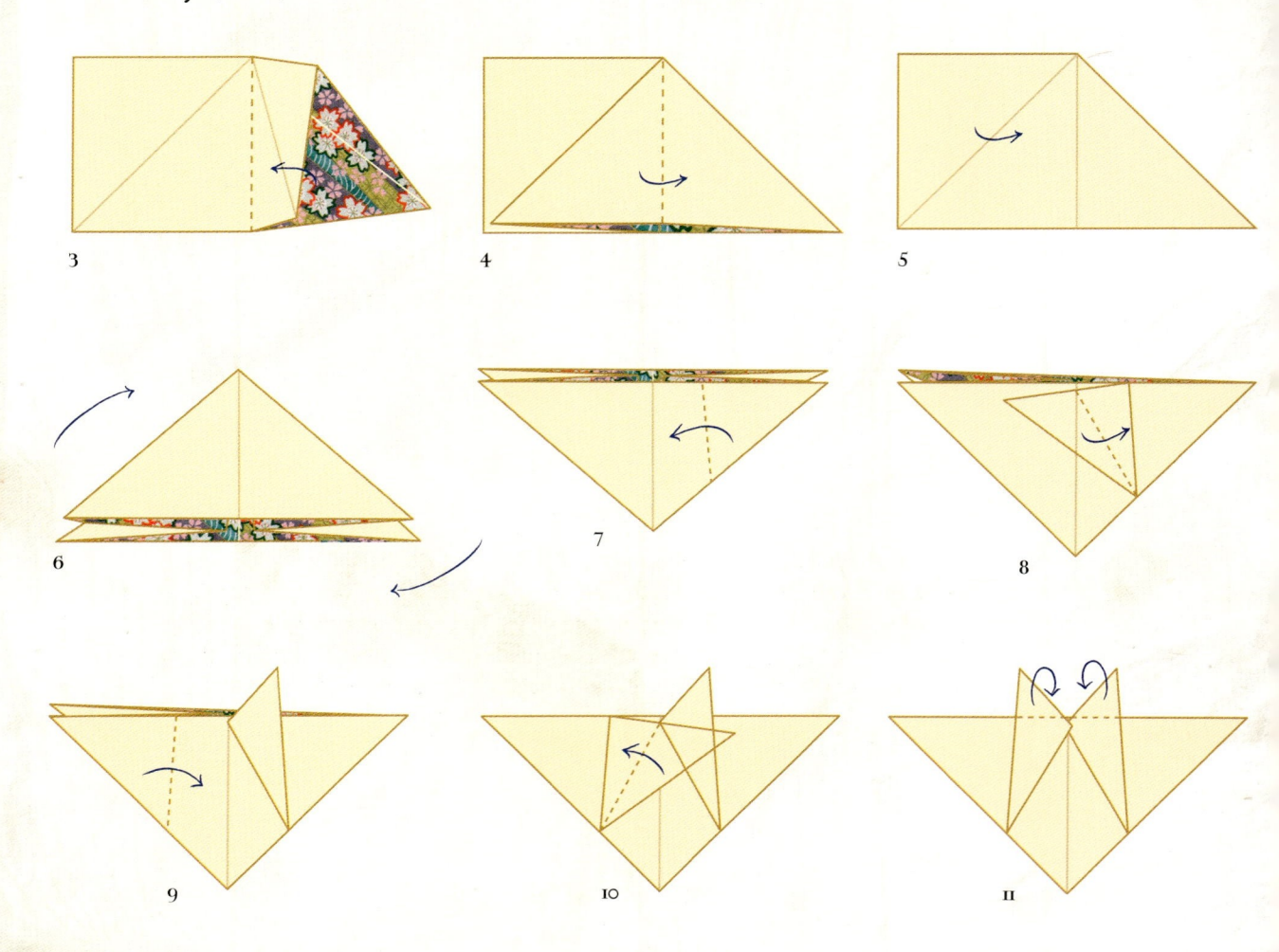

3. Lift the right-hand point vertically, opening it towards you. Open the sides of the point with the help of the creases scored. Flatten, score the fold.
4. Fold the left-hand point to the right along the dotted line.
5. Turn the top left-hand point back again towards the right along the dotted line. Repeat steps 3 to 5.
6. Score the folds. Pivot the folding upside down.
7. Fold along the dotted line.
8. Fold along the dotted line.
9. Fold the left-hand point along the dotted line.
10. Fold along the dotted line.
11. Turn the points over inside the folding.

celebrations

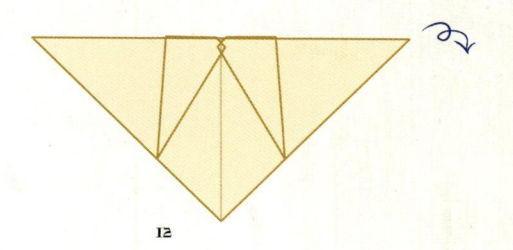

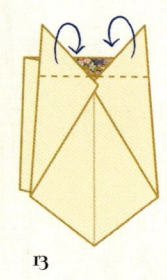

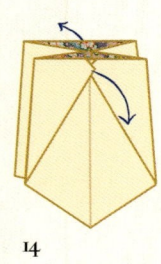

12. Turn the folding over. Repeat steps 7 to 10.
13. Fold the points over inside the folding.
14. Open out into the bag shape.

assembly

Open the flaps of the bag. Pierce two holes on either side of the flaps level with the fold as shown. Thread in the white cord. Spread glue on the flaps and glue them to the inside of the bag. Hold in place while the adhesive dries. Repeat the process with the other side of the bag. Cut out the decorative paper tab using the motif and dimensions below and glue a hole-punched shape on to the front. Glue the tab on the bag to close it.

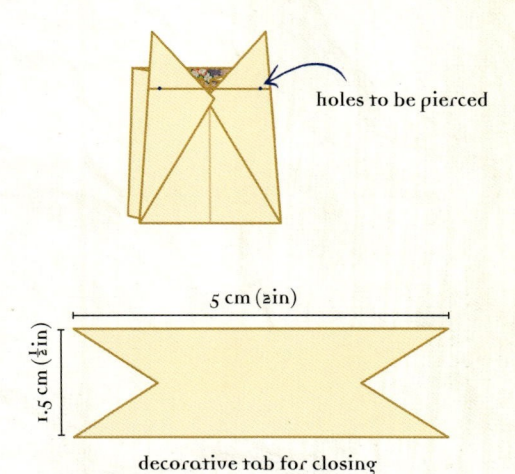

holes to be pierced

5 cm (2in)
1.5 cm (½in)

decorative tab for closing
the bag, shown at
actual size

118

celebrations

wedding flowers

difficulty ♦♦♦

MATERIALS FOR 21 FLOWERS
7 squares of 12 x 12cm (4¾ x 4¾in) white Ingres paper ♦ 7 squares of 12 x 12cm (4¾ x 4¾in) white paper with gold dust ♦ 7 squares of 12 x 12cm (4¾ x 4¾) beige paper with gold dust ♦ florist's wire ♦ masking tape

EQUIPMENT
1 paper folder ♦ 1 pair of scissors ♦ 1 pair of cutting pliers ♦ 1 pencil ♦ 1 embroidery needle ♦ ribbon

folding

1. Fold the centre lines then the diagonals of the square along the dotted lines. Unfold.
2. Fold the square in half along the diagonal.
3. Lift the top point vertically, opening it towards you.

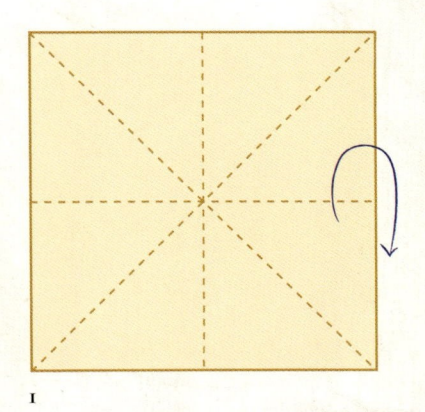

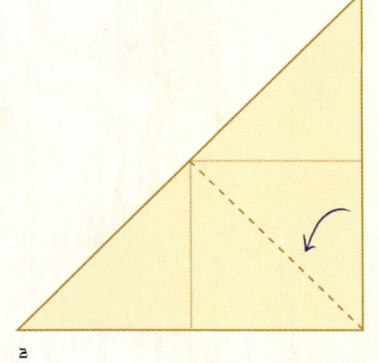

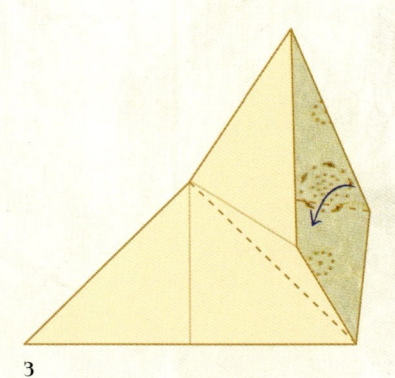

wedding flowers (cont.)

4. Open the sides of the point with the help of the creases scored.
5. Turn the entire paper folding over to the reverse side.
6. Repeat steps 3 to 5 folding over the right-hand point.
7. Score the folds and rotate.
8. Fold along the diagonals. Unfold.
9. Lift the far right-hand triangle. Open it out and flatten. Score the folds.
10. Fold the folding in half along the dotted line. Unfold.
11. Fold along the dotted lines and score the folds.
12. Unfold.
13. Open by pulling towards you, folding the point over towards the bottom. Score the folds.

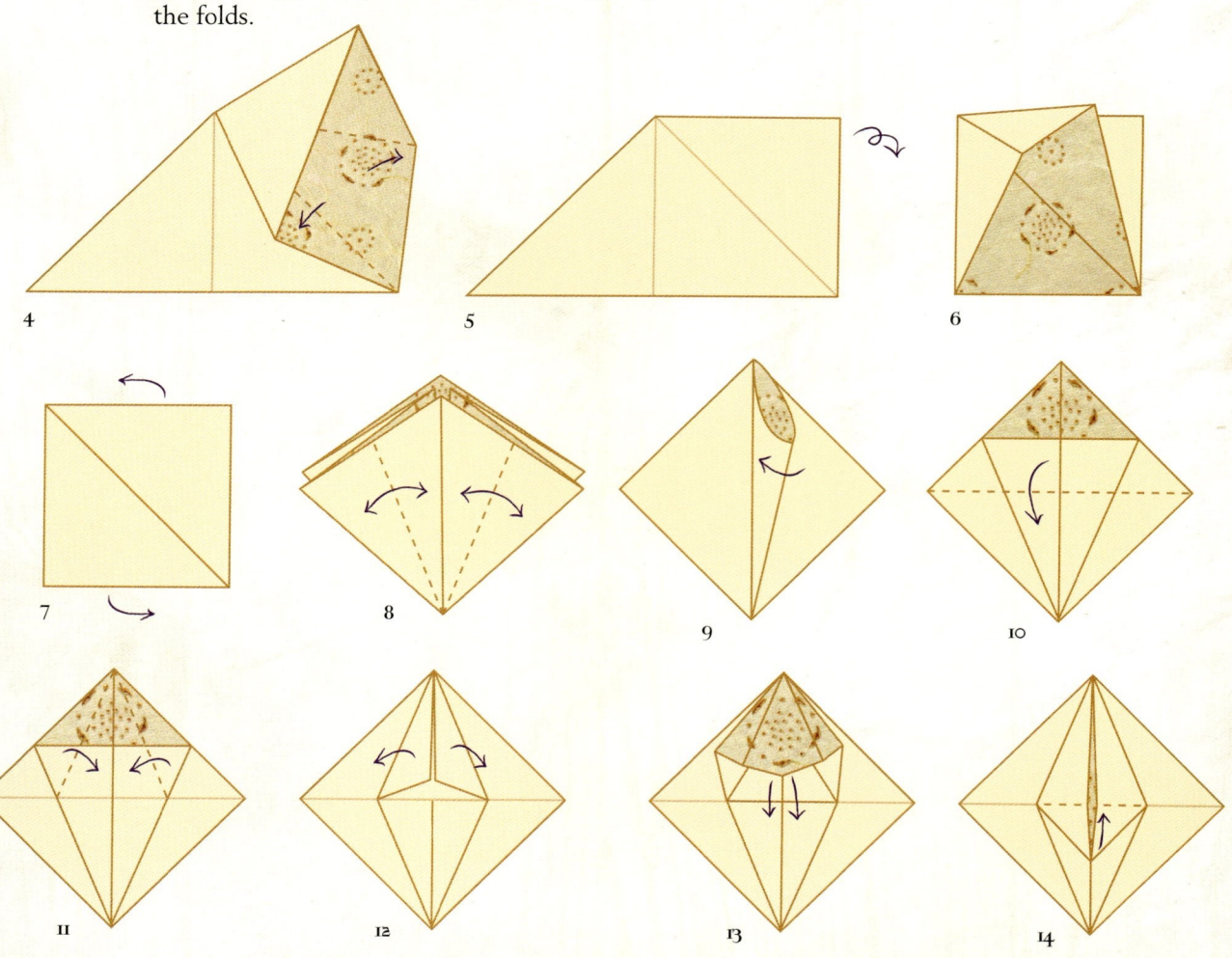

celebrations

14. Fold along the dotted line, turning the point up towards the top.
15. Fold over the left-hand wing of the diamond towards the right along the dotted line.
16. Fold over the left-hand wing again to obtain a square.
17. Repeat steps 8 to 16. Repeat the process for all the wings until the folding resembles a diamond, then fold the last left-hand wing over to the right.
18. Fold the two wings of the first diamond along the dotted lines. Fold the right-hand wing over to the left. Fold the right-hand wing over again to the left to obtain a large diamond. Repeat the process to the last wing.
19. Score the fold of the first petal along the dotted line.
20. Gently open the flower and score the folds of each petal. Bend the petals over to the outside of the flower curling them around a pencil.

folding

Using a pair of cutting pliers, cut one piece of florist's wire per flower. Pierce the centre of the flowers using an embroidery needle. Slide in the florist's wire and secure it by wrapping the base of the flower with masking tape. Use ribbon to tie the wire stems of the flowers together in small bouquets.

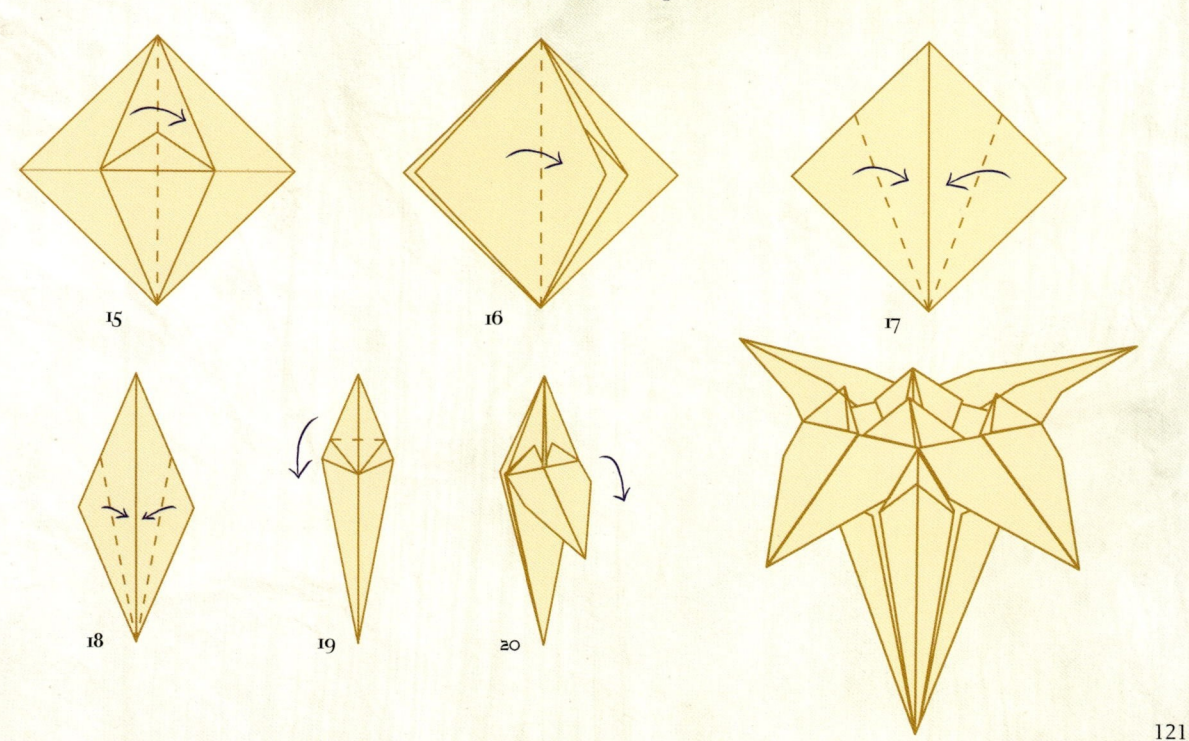

15

16

17

18

19

20

121

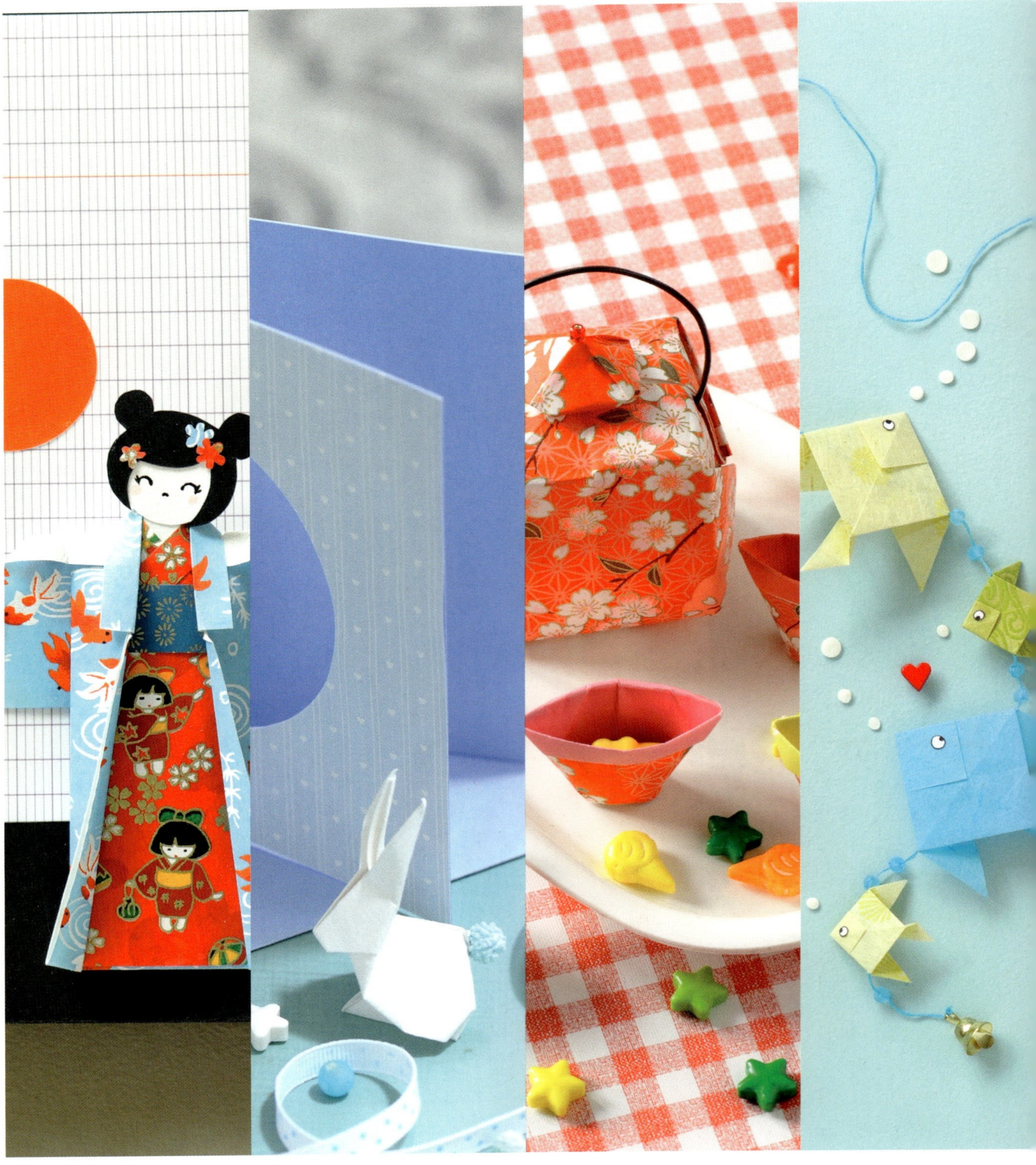

for children

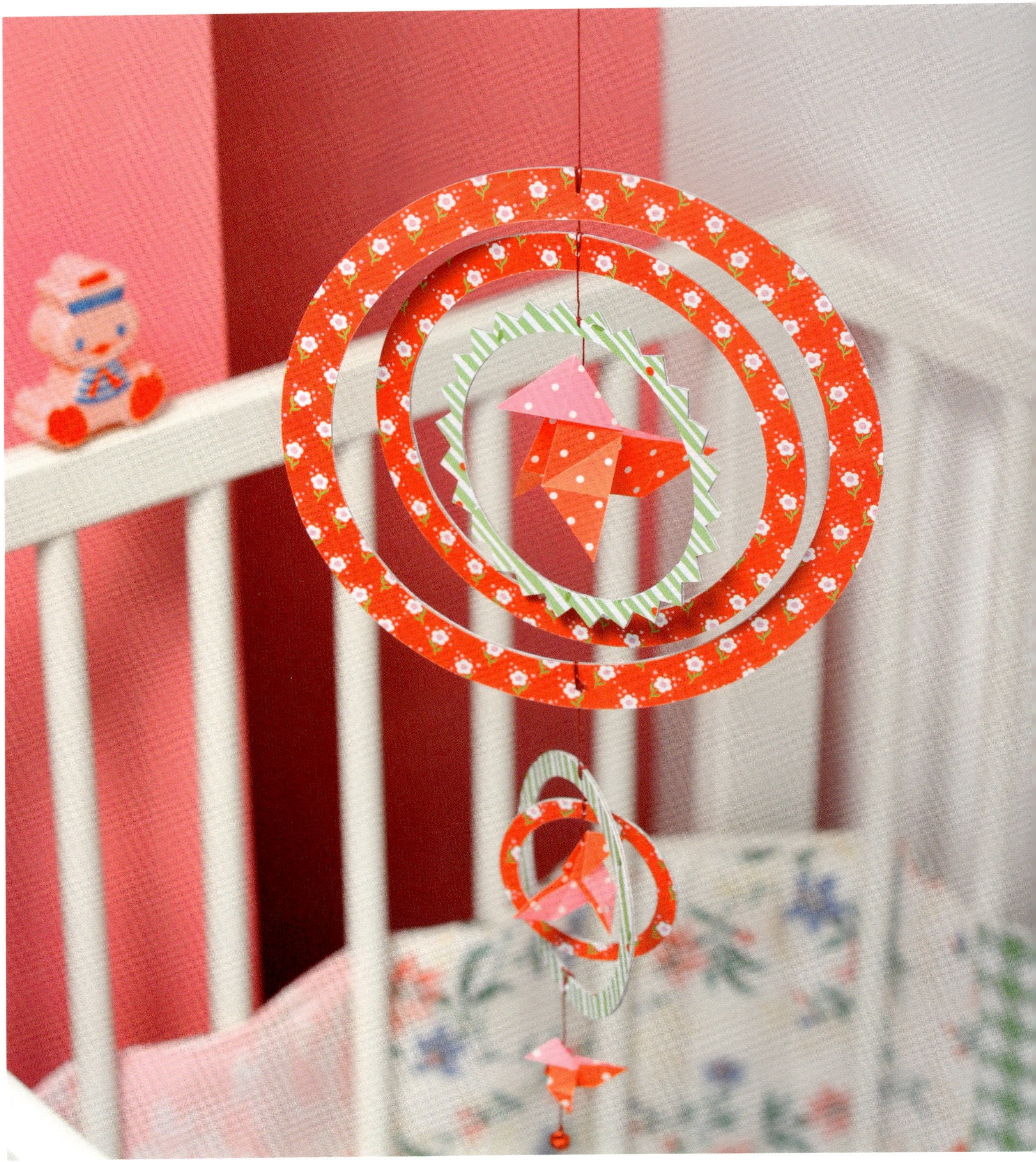

for children

baby's bird mobile

difficulty ♦♦

MATERIAL FOR ONE MOBILE
3 sheets of paper in matching patterns 22 x 30cm (8¾ x 11¾in) ♦ 1 piece of 5mm thick card 22 x 30cm (8¾ x 11¾in) ♦ 1 square of double-sided, spotted origami paper 9 x 9cm (3½ x 3½in) ♦ 1 square of double-sided, spotted origami paper 5 x 5cm (2 x 2in) ♦ 1 square of double-sided, spotted origami paper 3 x 3cm (1¼ x 1¼in) ♦ red cotton thread ♦ 1 little red bell

EQUIPMENT
1 paper folder ♦ 1 tapestry needle ♦ 1 craft knife ♦ 1 cutting mat ♦ 1 tube of gel adhesive ♦ 1 pair of scissors ♦ 1 compass

folding

1. Fold the sheet in half. Unfold.
2. Fold the two halves along the dotted lines and flatten.
3. Fold along the dotted line. Unfold.
4. Fold along the dotted lines.
5. Fold each point along the dotted lines.

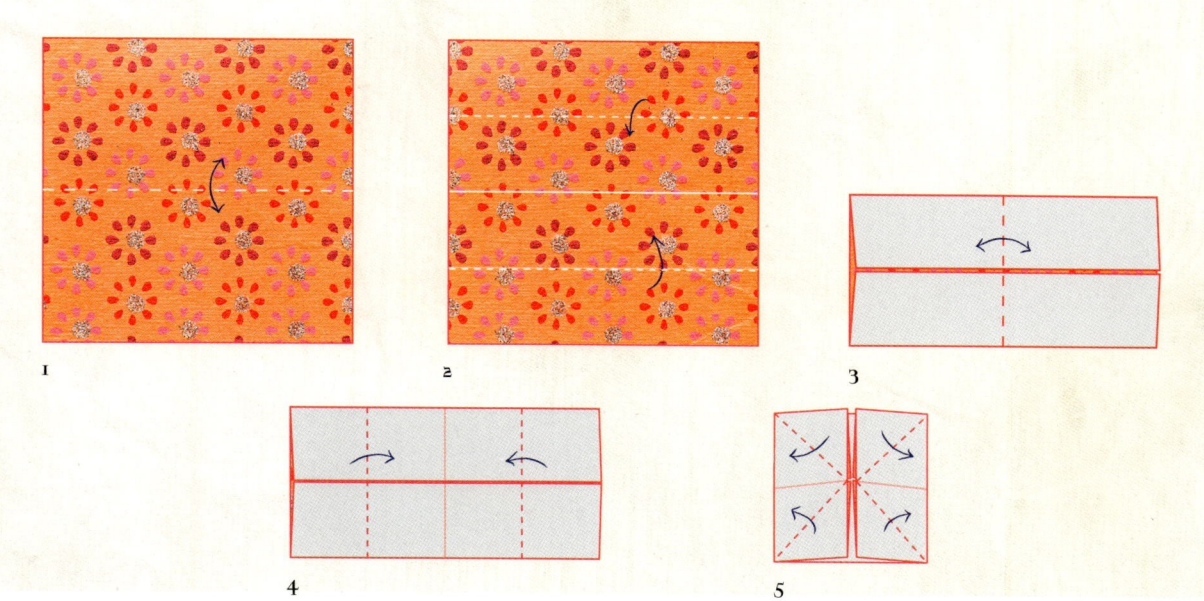

baby's bird mobile (cont.)

6. Unfold to reveal the strip from step 3. Fold the diagonals along the dotted lines. Unfold.
7. Open the right-hand side of the folding.
8. Fold over with the help of the creases indicated by the dotted lines. Flatten well.
9. Repeat the process with the left-hand side.
10. Pivot the folding by a quarter turn in the direction of the arrows.
11. Fold along the dotted line to bring the point to the top.
12. Fold in half to the rear. The right-hand point will automatically stand up towards the top.
13. Pivot the folding by a quarter turn in the direction of the arrows.
14. Open the folding at the top point. Invert the fold indicated along the dotted line. Close the folding and score the folds.

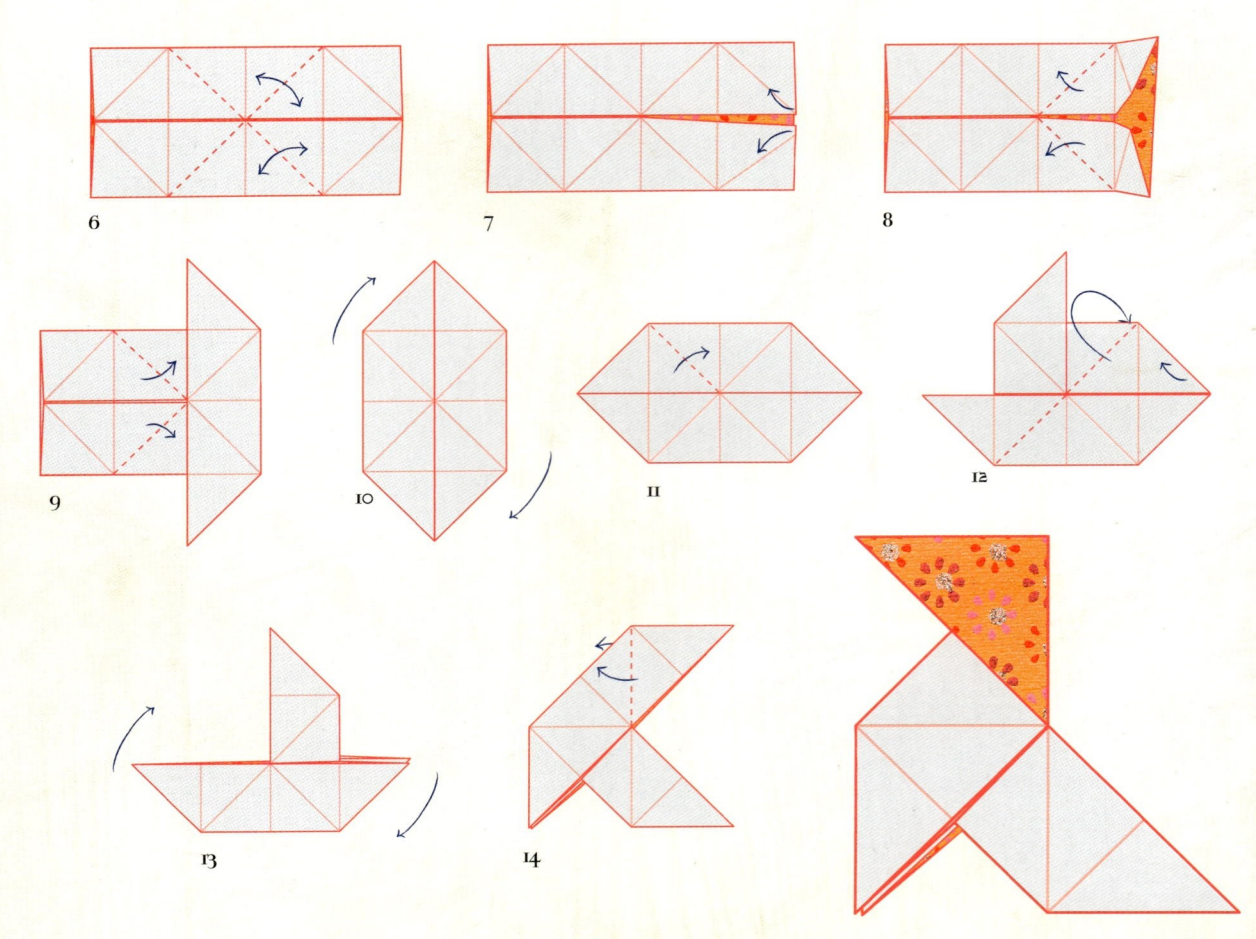

for children

assembly

Make three birds following the folding instructions.

Take a compass and draw the rings of the mobile on to a piece of thick card using the dimensions below. Cut out with the craft knife on a cutting mat.

To cover the rings, take two sheets of matching patterned paper. Spread adhesive on one of the faces of the largest ring and cover with the paper. Smooth out with your hand. Leave to dry. Cut off the excess paper with the craft knife following the edge of the card carefully. Proceed in the same way when covering the other side of the ring with a second sheet of paper. Cover all of the rings. Using a tapestry needle, pierce holes in the rings as shown on the template, so that they can be suspended.

Take a piece of thread, make a knot in one end, then thread a needle. Make a hole behind the largest bird's head so that it can be suspended. Pass the thread through the bird. Attach it to the largest ring. Assemble the rings from largest to smallest, as in the templates. Add the three birds. Attach a little red bell to the bottom of the mobile. Finish off by attaching a thread to the top so that the mobile can be suspended.

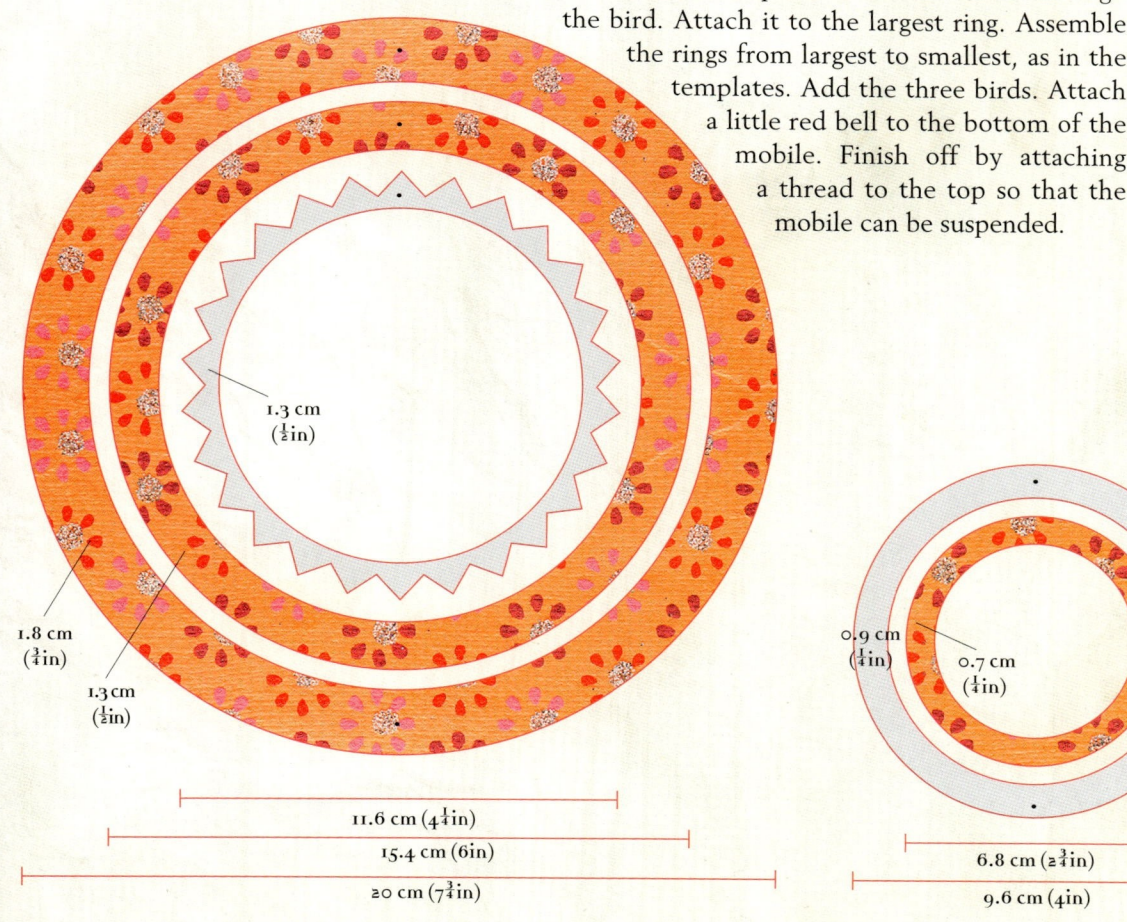

1.3 cm ($\frac{1}{2}$in)

1.8 cm ($\frac{3}{4}$in)

1.3 cm ($\frac{1}{2}$in)

0.9 cm ($\frac{1}{4}$in)

0.7 cm ($\frac{1}{4}$in)

11.6 cm ($4\frac{1}{4}$in)

15.4 cm (6in)

20 cm ($7\frac{3}{4}$in)

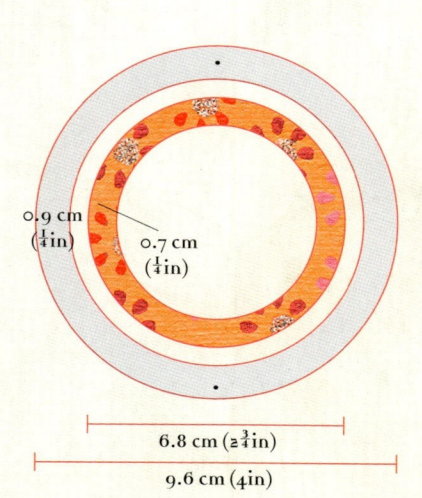

6.8 cm ($2\frac{3}{4}$in)

9.6 cm (4in)

128

for children

new baby card

difficulty ♦♦

MATERIALS FOR ONE CARD
1 blue card 15 x 30cm (6 x 11¾in) ♦ 1 rectangle of blue patterned paper 15 x 30cm (6 x 11¾in) ♦ 1 square of white Ingres paper 9 x 9cm (3½ x 3½in) ♦ white metallic thread

EQUIPMENT
1 paper folder ♦ 1 tapestry needle ♦ 1 craft knife ♦ 1 cutting mat ♦ 1 tube of gel adhesive ♦ 1 pair of scissors ♦ clips ♦ 1 compass

folding

1. Take the white Ingres paper and fold it in half. Score the fold and unfold.
2. Fold the two halves along the dotted lines. Unfold. Pivot by a quarter turn towards the right.
3. Fold in half. Score the fold and unfold.

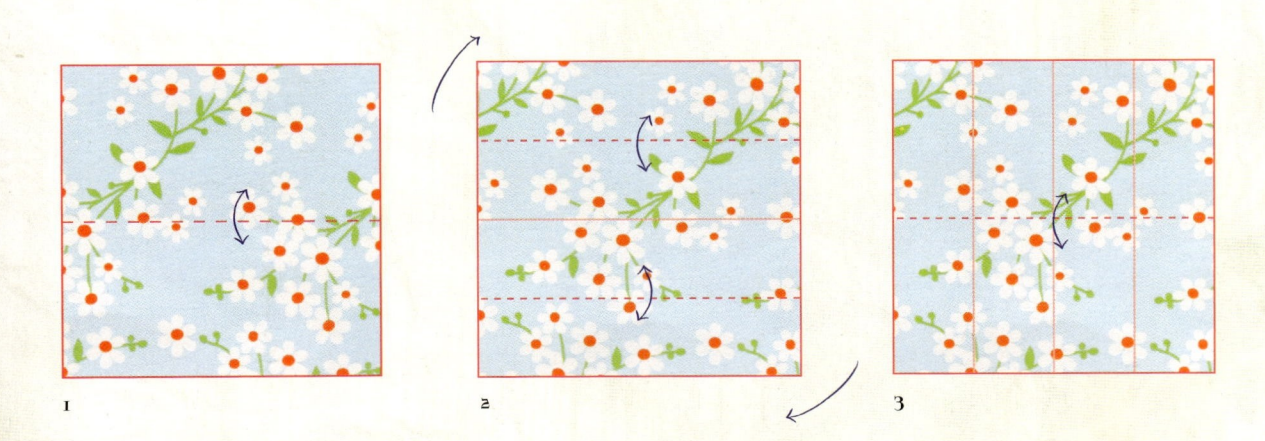

1   2   3

new baby card (cont.)

4. Fold the two halves along the dotted lines.
5. Fold the corners along the dotted lines. Unfold.
6. Open the bottom right corner.
7. Fold along the dotted lines to open fully.
8. Flatten and repeat the process with the top corner.
9. Repeat steps 6 to 8 with the left-hand corner. Flatten. Turn the folding over.
10. Fold along the dotted lines.
11. Fold along the dotted line.
12. Pull out the bottom point to stand out naturally and fold the left-hand point.
13. Fold in half towards the rear lengthways.
14. Hold on to the points of the ears and lift upwards. Flatten.
15-16. Open the points at the rear of the rabbit.
17. Push the points inside the body making them come out at the front and form the paws. Flatten.
18. Fold the points at the rear of the rabbit inside the body. Flatten.

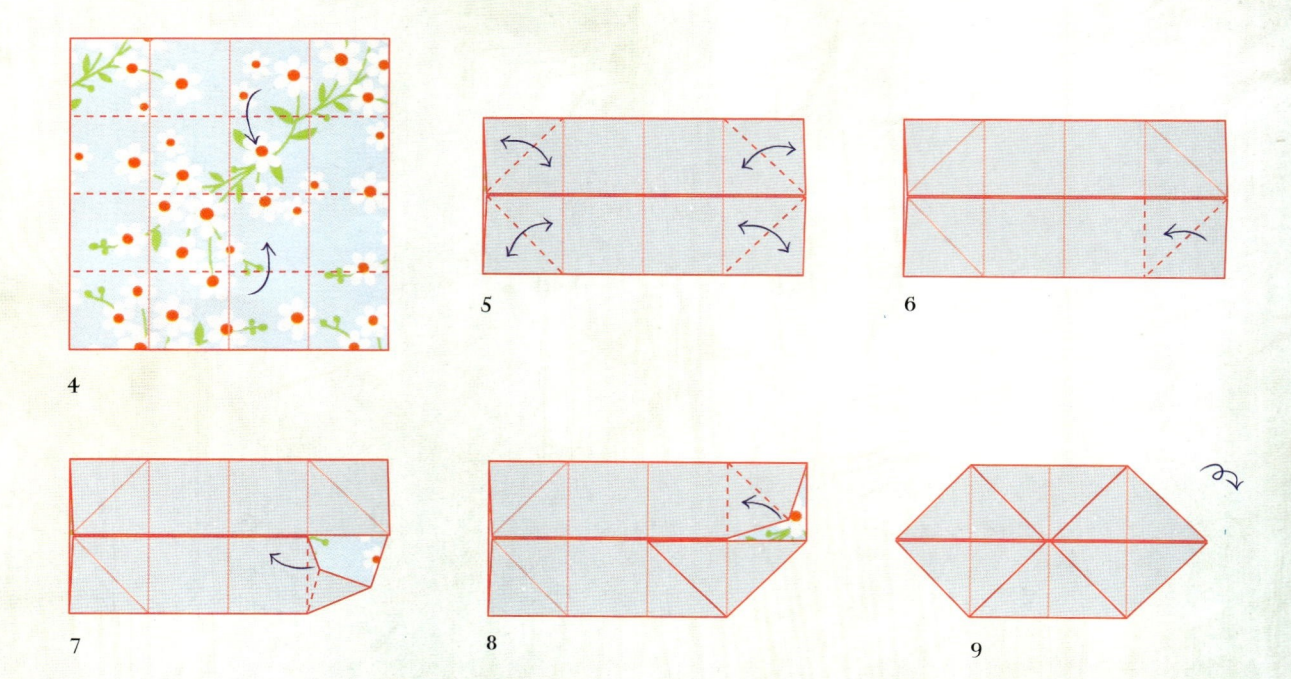

for children

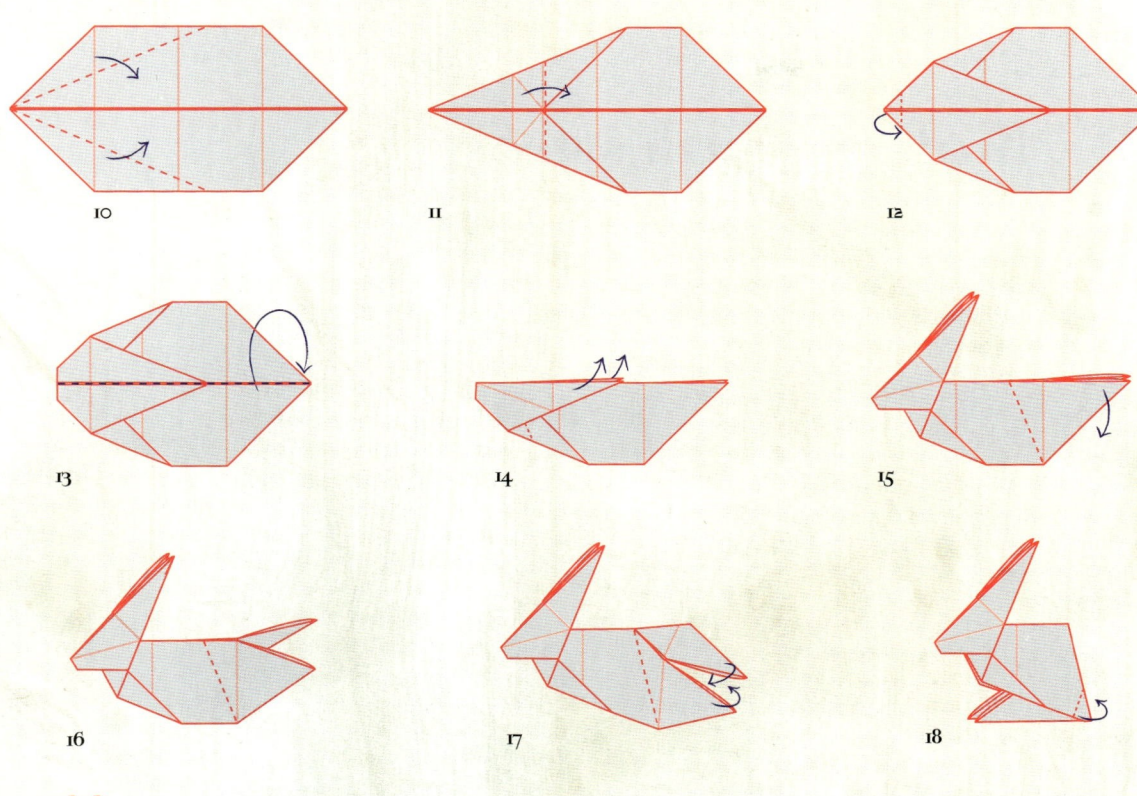

assembly

Pierce the body of the rabbit, vertically, through its centre from the top to bottom using a tapestry needle. Thread a needle with the white metallic thread. Knot one end of the thread and pass it through the body of the rabbit so that it can be suspended.

Fold the blue card in half and cover it in blue patterned paper without glueing it. Secure with clips.

On the inside of the front surface of your card, trace two diagonal lines and mark the centre where the diagonals intersect. Put the point of a compass at the intersection and draw a circle 8cm (3¼in) in diameter. On a cutting mat, cut out the centre with the craft knife. Glue the thread that suspends the rabbit between the edges of the paper and the card in the top centre of the circle. Secure the thread using a spot of adhesive and a little piece of paper. Now glue the paper to the card using the gel adhesive. Smooth with your hand. Leave to dry.

for children

birdcage with sweets   difficulty ♦♦

MATERIALS FOR ONE BIRDCAGE
1 square of white Washi paper 12 x 12cm (4¾ x 4¾in) ♦ 1 strip of 200gsm (135lbs) white paper 3 x 27cm (1¼ x 10¾in) ♦ 1 sheet of thin card 21 x 29.7cm (8¼ x 11¾in) ♦ 1 sheet of fuchsia pink paper 21 x 29.7cm (8¼ x 11¾in) ♦ 2 strips of patterned paper 3 x 27cm (1¼ x 10¾in) ♦ fuchsia pink cotton thread ♦ fuchsia pink aluminium wire ♦ craft tape ♦ fine card 21 x 29.7cm (8¼ x 11¾in)

EQUIPMENT
1 paper folder ♦ 1 tapestry needle ♦ 1 pair of scissors ♦ 1 pair of pliers for cutting the aluminium wire ♦ 1 pair of pliers ♦ 1 tube of adhesive ♦ 1 pencil ♦ 1 craft knife ♦ 1 cutting mat ♦ 1 ruler ♦ 1 compass

folding

1. Take the Washi paper and fold in half along the diagonal.
2. Pivot the folding towards the right.

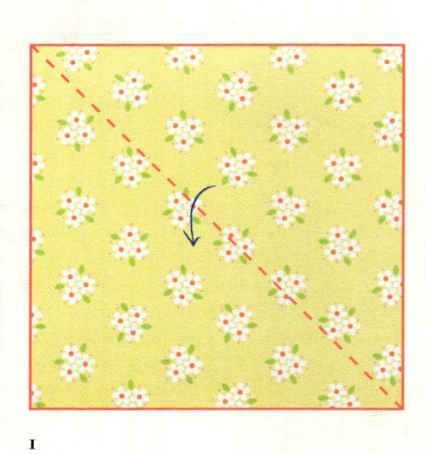

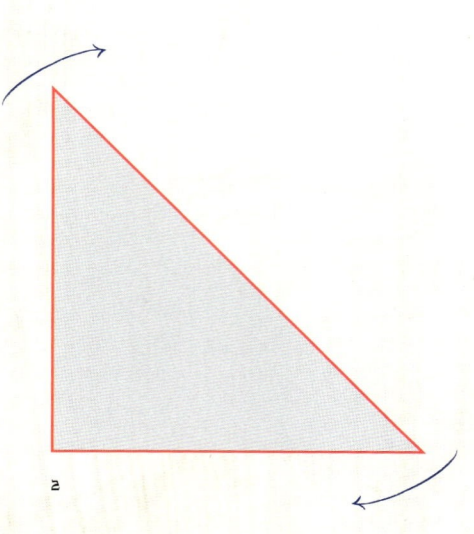

133

birdcage with sweets (cont.)

3. Fold along the dotted lines to fold the points up to the top.
4. Fold along the dotted line. Unfold.
5. Fold along the dotted lines.
6. Unfold.
7. Open the left-hand point. Push the point inside the folding.
8. Repeat the process with the right-hand point.
9. Fold in half towards the rear along the dotted line.
10. Fold the first sheet towards the bottom along the dotted line.
11. Flatten and turn the folding over.
12. Fold the first sheet towards the bottom along the dotted line.

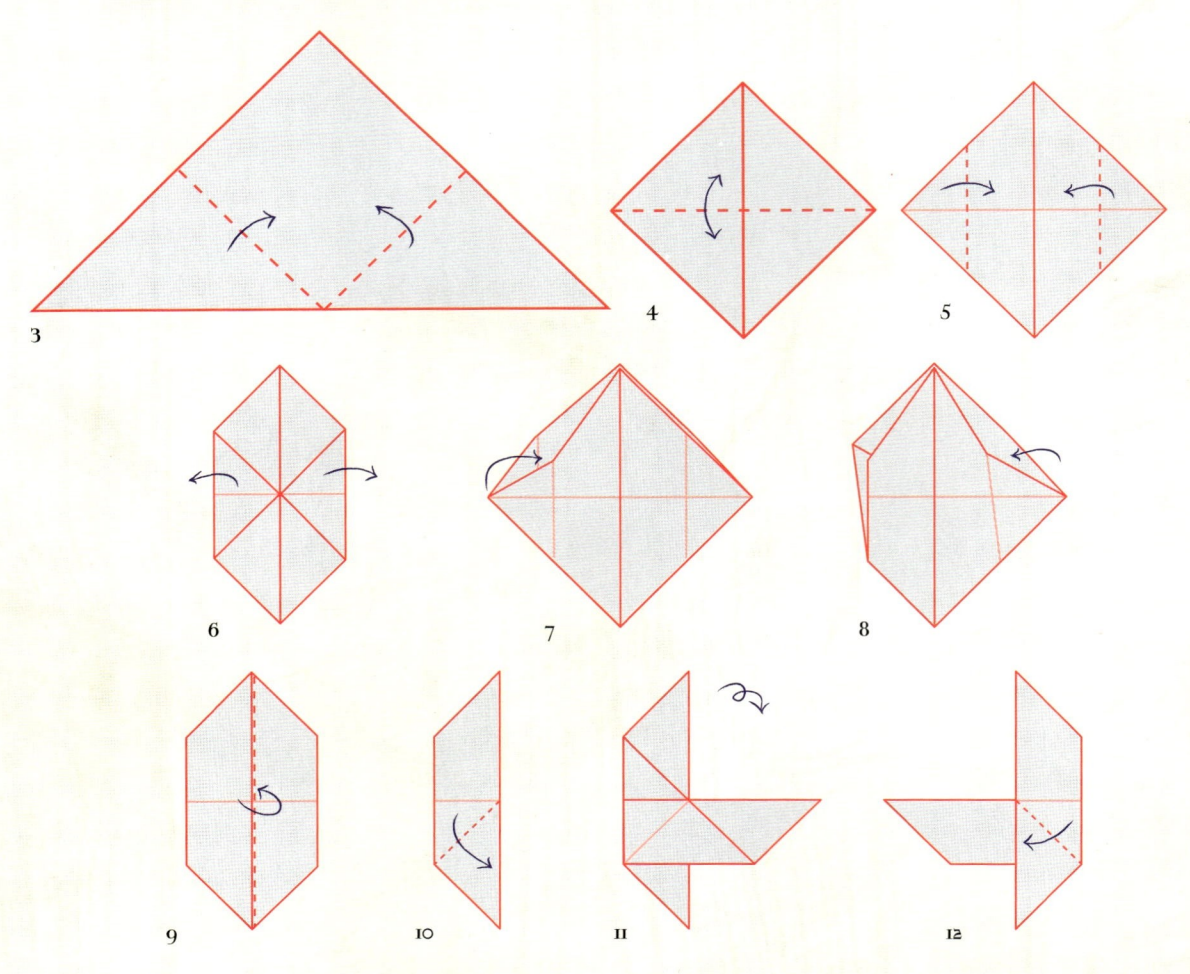

for children

13. Pivot the folding by a quarter turn to the right.
14. Fold along the dotted line.
15. Turn the folding over.
16. Fold along the dotted line.
17. Open the left-hand point and invert the fold downwards.
18. Fold along the dotted line to fold the point upwards.
19. Turn the folding over.
20. Fold along the dotted line to fold the point upwards.
21. Invert the fold along the dotted line to push the point into the folding.

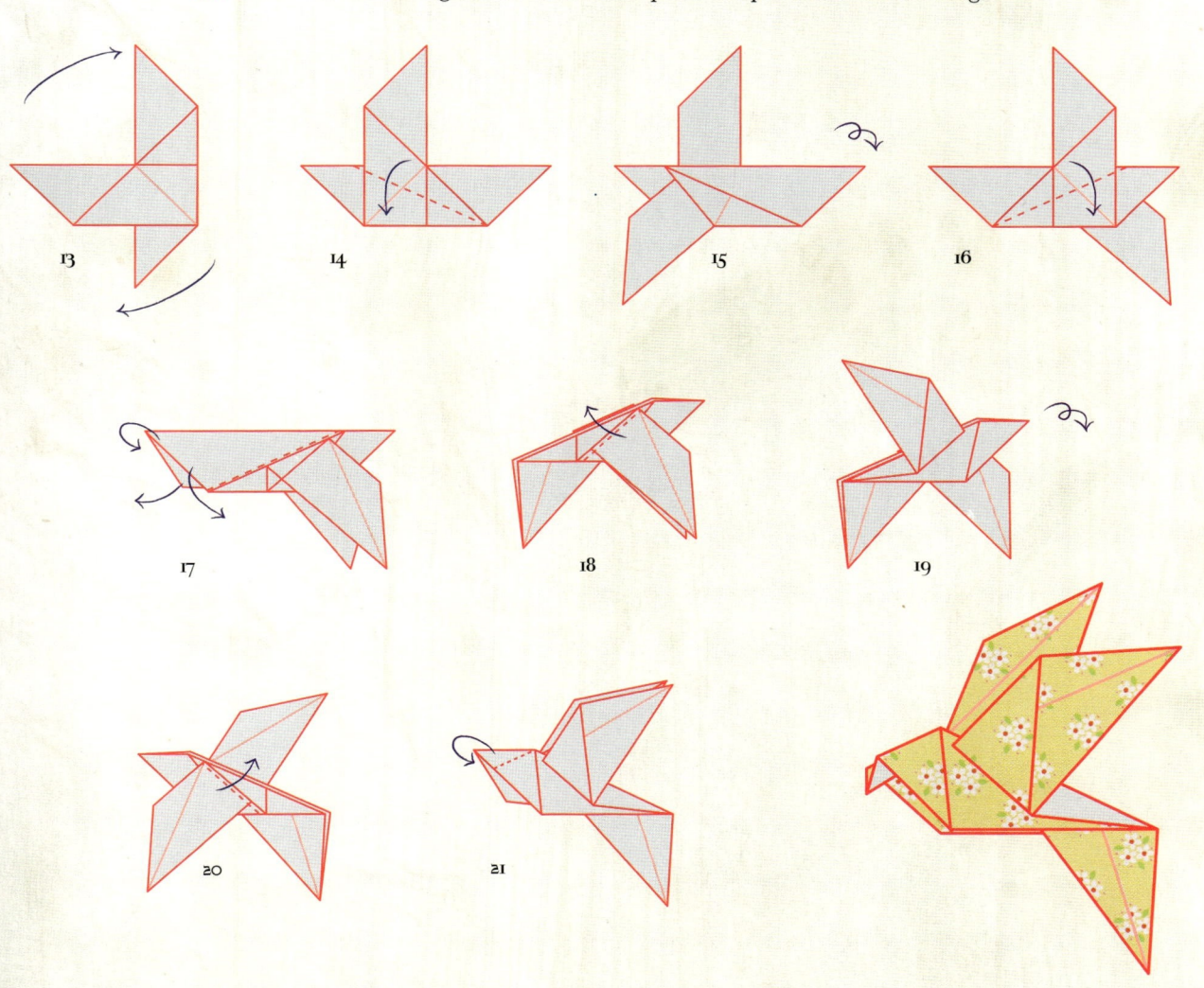

birdcage with sweets (cont.)

assembly

Using a compass, draw two circles 8cm (3¼in) in diameter on to the fine card and two more on the fuchsia pink paper. Cut out with a craft knife on a cutting mat.

Measure out three pieces of 30cm (11¾in) long fucshia pink aluminium wire. Cut with a pair of pliers. Measure another 35cm (13¾in) of wire. Cut. Cover each piece of card with a pink paper disc. Place the first disc with the pink side facing up.

Mark out the position of eight holes with a pencil using the diagram below. Pierce eight holes using a tapestry needle. Slide one end of the first aluminium wire into a hole. Bend the end back using a pair of pliers. Thread the other end through the opposite hole. Bend the end over. Secure beneath the card using craft tape.

Repeat the process for the two other wires. Make a heart in the middle of the longest wire and thread the ends into the remaining holes. Bend the ends over and secure with craft tape underneath the card disc. Glue the second card disc underneath the cage with the pink side facing downwards. Hold in place while the glue dries.

Wrap a piece of aluminium wire around the intersection of the wires to hold them in place. Adjust the bars of the cage so that they look nice. Draw six little flowers on patterned paper and cut out. Glue them in pairs to the bars of the cage.

Cut out a strip of white paper 3 x 27cm (1¼ x 10¾in). Cover with a new strip of patterned paper. Glue the strip around the base of the cage. Glue a second strip of patterned paper on top.

Using a tapestry needle, pierce a hole between the wings of the dove. Thread a needle with pink cotton. Knot one end. Thread the cotton into the dove. Attach the dove to the cage.

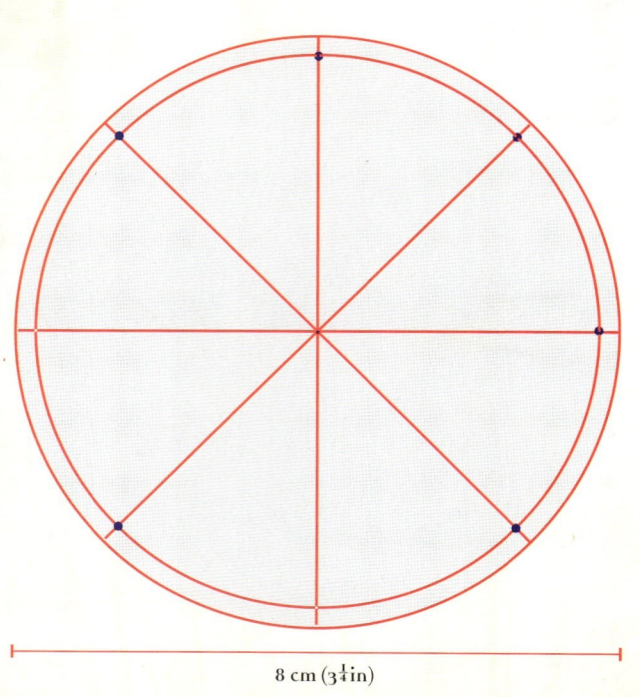

8 cm (3¼in)

for children

flowers
shown at actual size

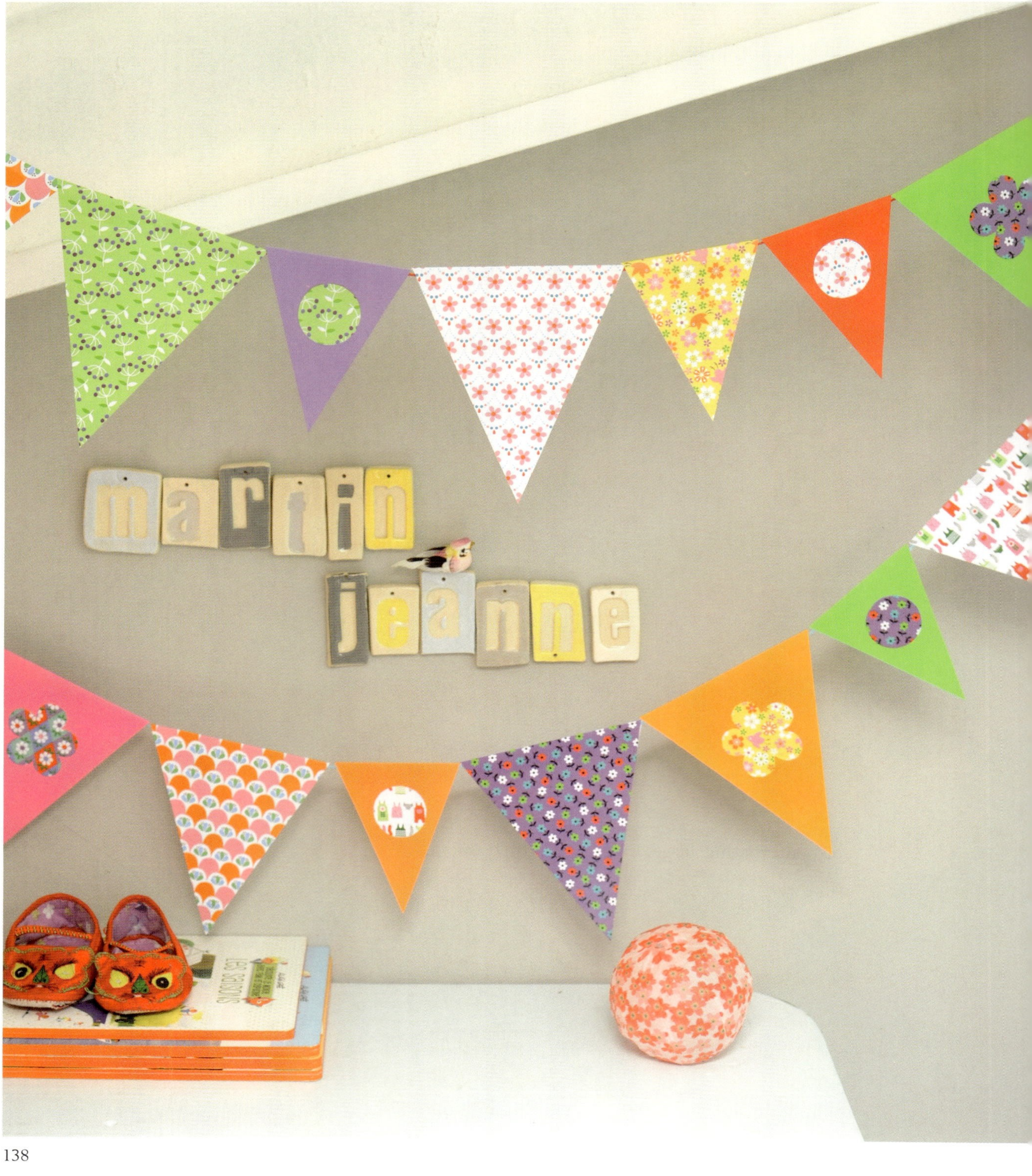
martin
jeanne
LES SAISONS

for children

bunting

difficulty ♦

MATERIALS FOR ONE LARGE GARLAND OR TWO SMALL GARLANDS
a selection of 8 patterned sheets 15cm x 15cm (6 x 6in) ♦ selection of 120g (4oz) plain sheets ♦ 1 sheet of thick paper

EQUIPMENT
1 craft knife ♦ 1 cutting mat ♦ 1 ruler ♦ 1 pair of scissors ♦ 1 pencil ♦ 1 tube of adhesive ♦ red cord

assembly

Trace the patterns for the flags from this page on to a piece of thick paper. Cut them out with the craft knife and ruler on a cutting mat. These will serve as templates.

Place the small template on the reverse of a piece of paper. Lightly draw around the edge with a pencil. Cut out with a craft knife and ruler on a cutting mat. Trace the flower and circle on to a piece of thick paper. Cut out with a pair of scissors to serve as templates. Place the templates on the reverse of patterned paper and lightly draw around the edges with a pencil. Cut out with a pair of scissors. Do the same to prepare the larger pennants.

Glue the flowers on to the large, plain pennants using a tube of adhesive. Glue the paper discs on to the small, plain pennants. Leave to dry. Score the folds of each pennant along the dotted line as indicated. Place the pennants right side down on the table, alternating large, small, patterned and plain, spacing them around 2cm (¾in) apart.

Place the red cord level with the fold. Apply a line of glue without touching the thread. Fold over the flaps. Hold together while the adhesive dries. Hang up the bunting.

enlarge to 125%

36 mm (1½in)

enlarge to 200%

enlarge to 200%

enlarge to 125%

for children

fishy garland

difficulty ♦♦

MATERIALS FOR ONE GARLAND OF SEVEN FISH
3 squares of matching, fine banana paper 7 x 7cm (2¾ x 2¾in) ♦ 4 squares of the same paper 3.5 x 3.5cm (1¼ x 1¼in) ♦ DMC no. 3845 royal blue special stranded cotton thread 60 to 70cm (23½ x 27½in) ♦ 1 little bell 1cm (½in) diameter ♦ blue glass beads 4mm in diameter

EQUIPMENT
1 paper folder ♦ 1 tapestry needle ♦ 1 pair of scissors ♦ 1 tube of adhesive ♦ 1 pencil ♦ black fine felt-tip pen ♦ 1 craft knife ♦ 1 cutting mat ♦ 1 ruler

folding

1. Fold the sheet in half along the dotted lines to score the centre lines and unfold. Score the folds of the diagonals. Fold the left-hand corner in towards the centre.
2. Score the fold and turn the entire folding over.

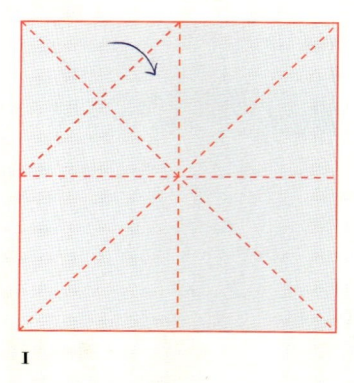

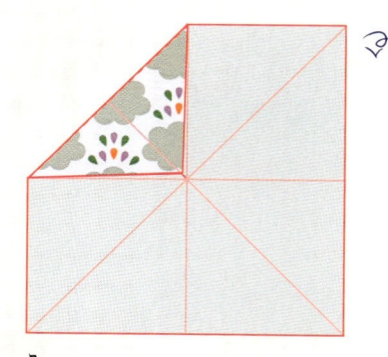

141

fishy garland (cont.)

3. Fold the two sides towards the centre along the dotted lines shown.
4. Fold along the dotted lines towards the centre. Unfold.
5. Score the folds for the diagonals indicated along the dotted line. Unfold.
6. Score the folds for the diagonals indicated along the dotted line. Unfold.
7. Fold along the dotted lines and open the two lower points from the centre to the outside. Flatten the folds.
8. Separate the top centre point by opening it to the right and fold along the dotted line.
9. Fold the two lower outside points down to the bottom along the dotted lines.
10. Fold the point over along the dotted line.
11. Score the fold. Turn the fish over. Draw on the eye of the fish with a fine, black felt-tip pen.

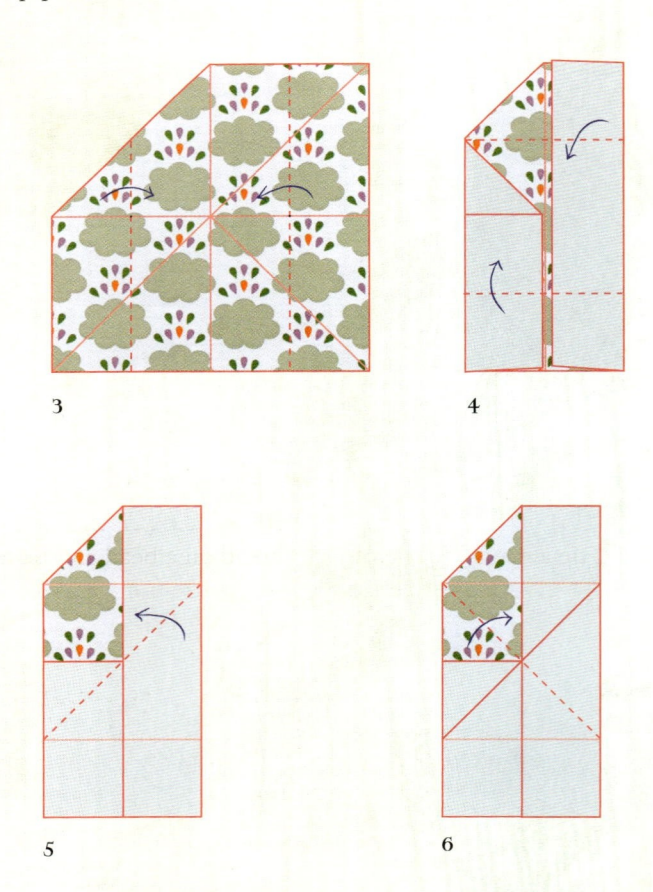

for children

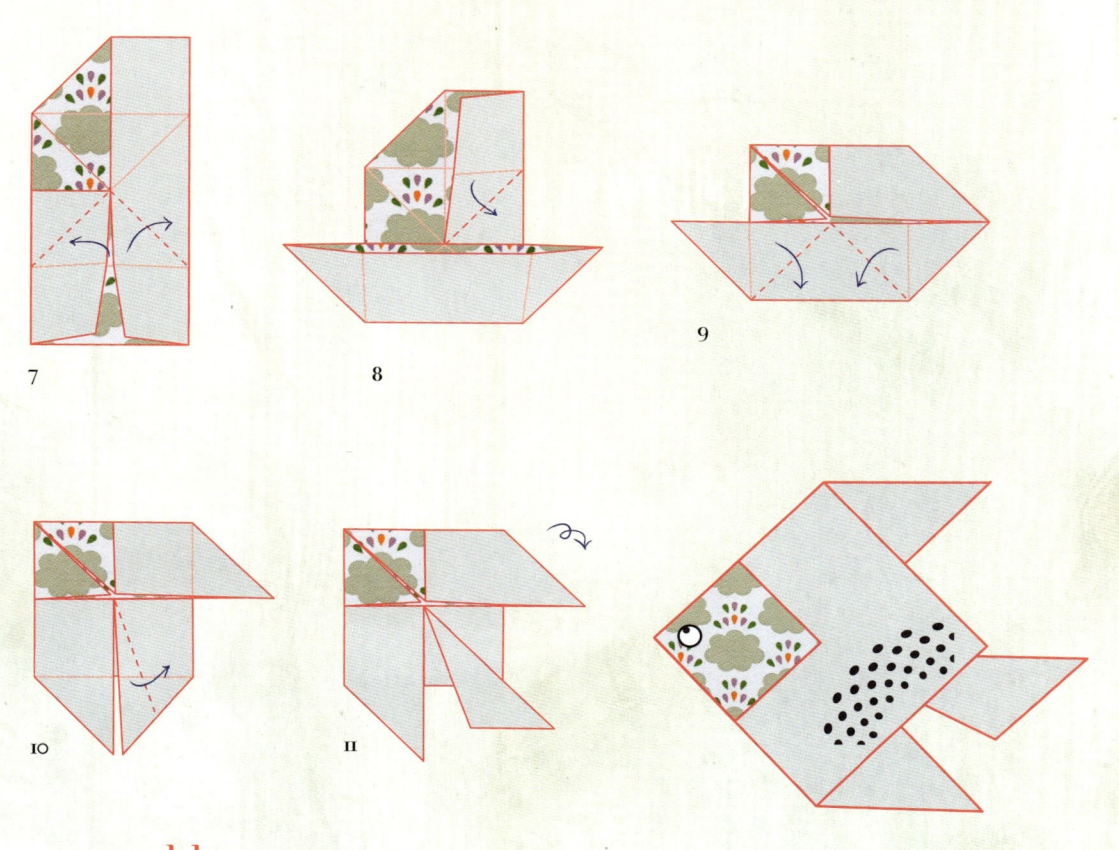

assembly

Make three large fish and four little fish using the diagrams for the folding.

Cut one piece of royal blue stranded cotton around 70cm (27½in) long. Tie a little bell to one end and tie a needle to the other. Thread on a bead and tie a knot next to it, keeping it in place at the bottom. Thread one little fish on to the needle and gently slide it along the thread until it reaches the bead, leaving a gap of around 1cm (½in) between the two.

Next add two knotted beads leaving irregular gaps between the items. Slide on a large fish, then two beads knotted in place, a little fish and then three beads and so on until the garland is complete. Remove the needle, make a loop at the end of the thread and tie with a knot for hanging the garland.

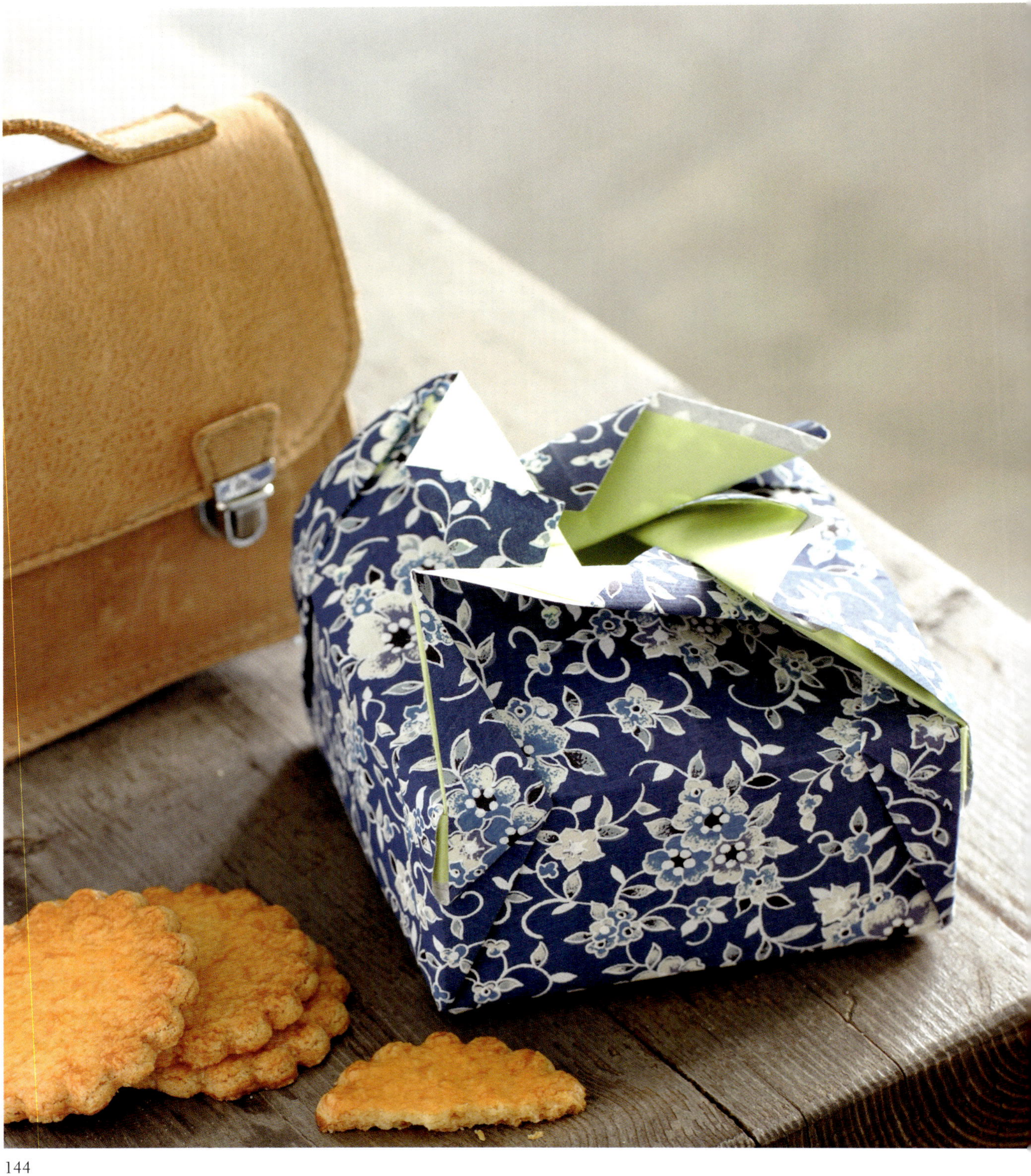

for children

little savouries box

difficulty ♦♦

MATERIALS FOR ONE BOX
1 sheet of patterned origami paper 25 x 25cm (9¾ x 9¾in) ♦ 1 sheet of plain origami paper 24 x 24cm (9½ x 9½in) ♦ 1 sheet of greaseproof paper 22 x 22cm (8¾ x 8¾in)

EQUIPMENT
1 craft knife ♦ 1 cutting mat ♦ 1 ruler ♦ 1 paper folder ♦ 1 tube of adhesive ♦ set square

folding

1. Glue the origami paper to the square of plain paper. Score the centre lines and the diagonals. Fold to the rear along the diagonal.
2. Score the fold along the dotted line and unfold.

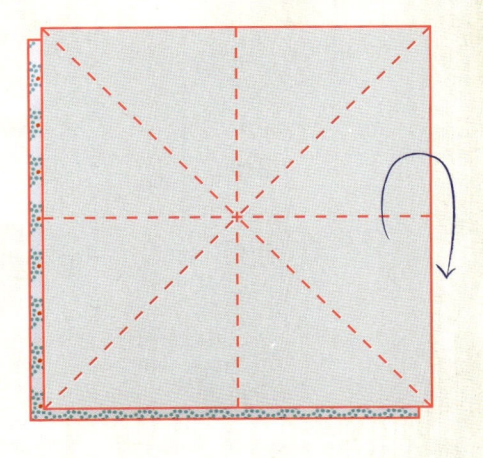

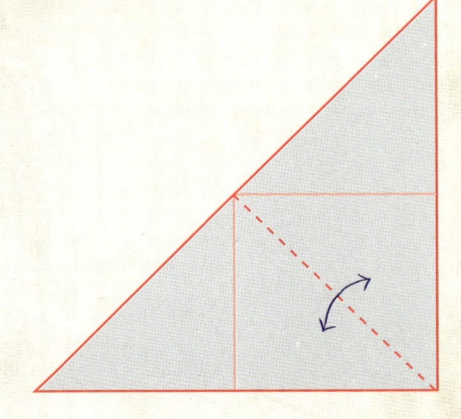

little savouries box (cont.)

3. Lift the top point towards you.
4. Flatten down the new fold allowing the edges to open out and form a new square.
5. Flip the entire folding over to its reverse side as shown.
6. Repeat steps 3 to 5 with the remaining point to form another square. Flatten the folds.
7. Pivot the folding in the direction of the arrows as shown.
8. Fold the points to the centre along the dotted lines.
9. Flatten the folding.
10. Open the left-hand point at the centre of the folding.
11. Centre it to obtain a diamond shape. Flatten.
12. Repeat the process with the right-hand point at the centre.
13. Fold along the dotted lines.
14. Unfold.
15. Open the folds towards the bottom, along the dotted lines.
16. Pull the folds towards the bottom and fold the sides over towards the centre.
17. Fold the lozenges to the rear along their centres. Turn the folding over.
18. Repeat steps 10 to 17.

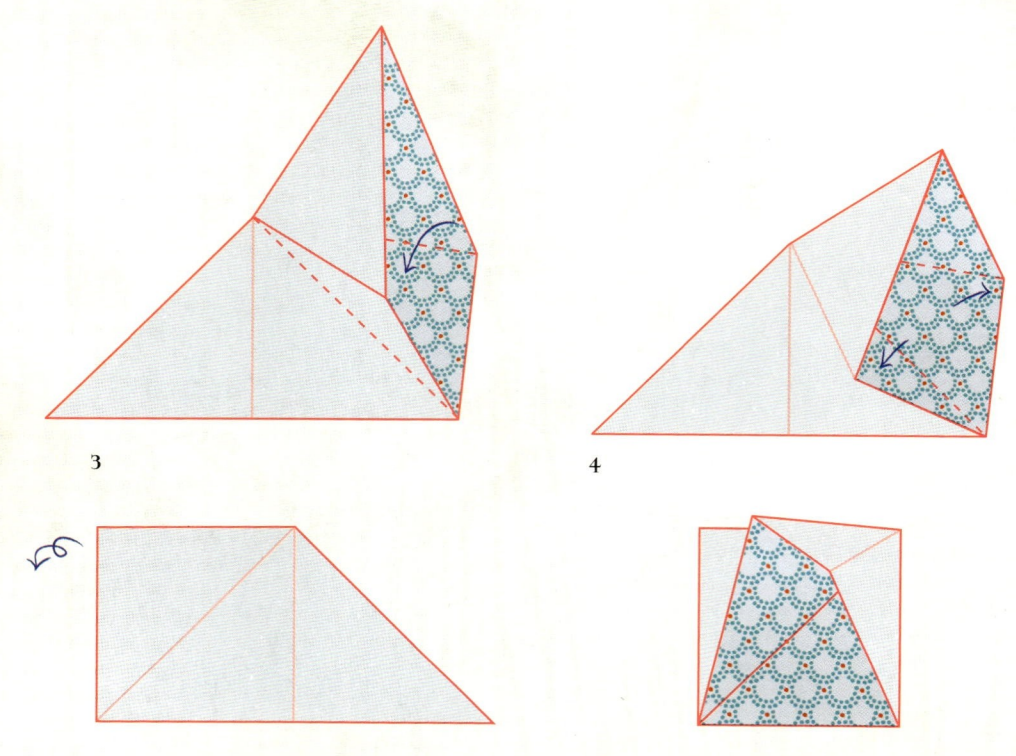

3

4

5

6

for children

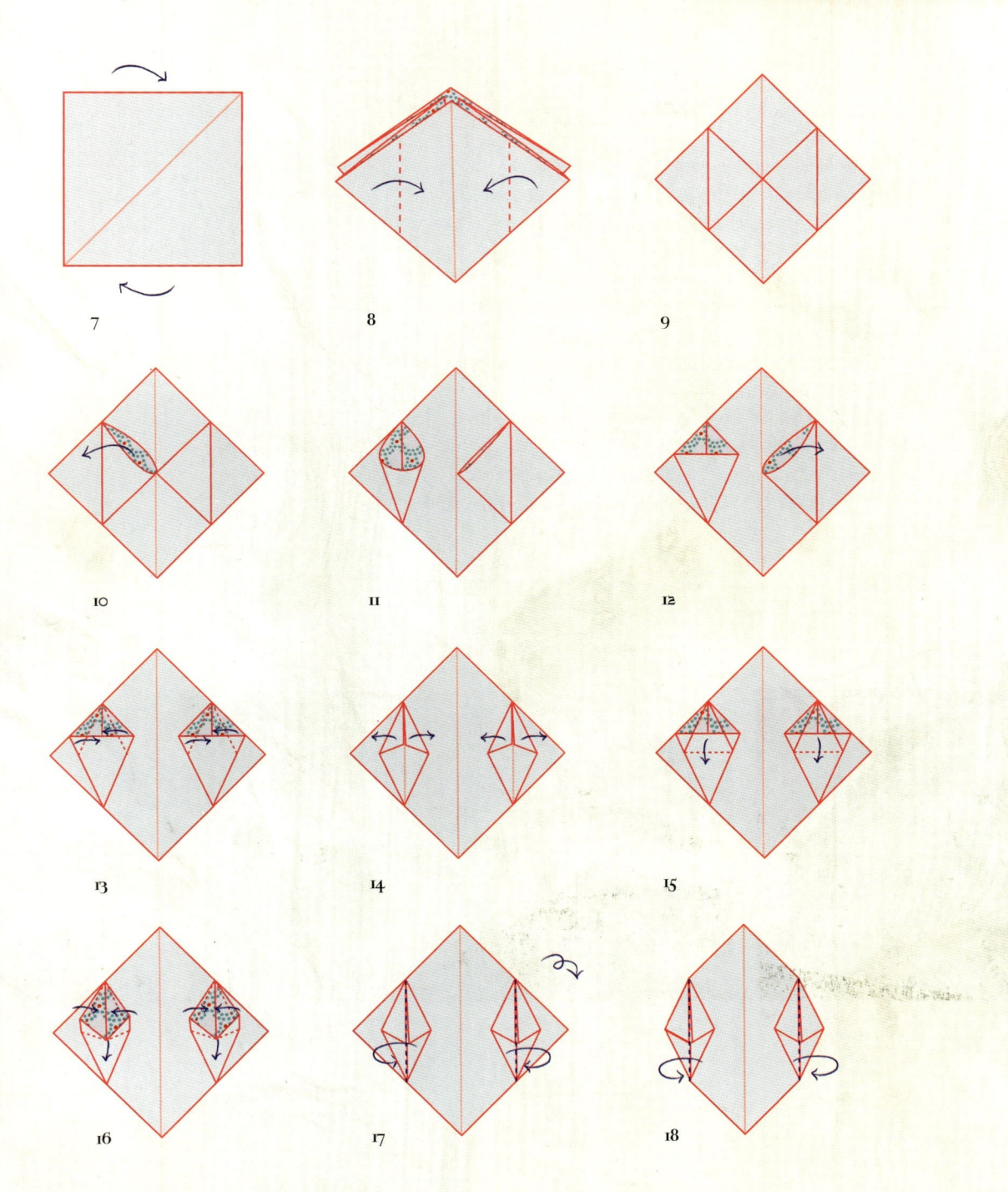

7

8

9

10

11

12

13

14

15

16

17

18

147

little savouries box (cont.)

19. Fold along the dotted line. Unfold.
20. Fold the first thickness along the dotted line.
21. Fold along the dotted line to fold over the point of the first sheet towards the centre.
22. Fold along the dotted line.
23. Fold the first sheet over towards the left along the dotted line and then repeat steps 20 to 22 for each of the top points until the box resembles diagram 24.
24. Carefully open the folding from the centre to give the box its shape, pulling up the base to form a flat surface.
25. Fold the points of the box to the rear along the dotted lines.
26. Fold along the dotted lines folding the points over towards the centre.

for childen

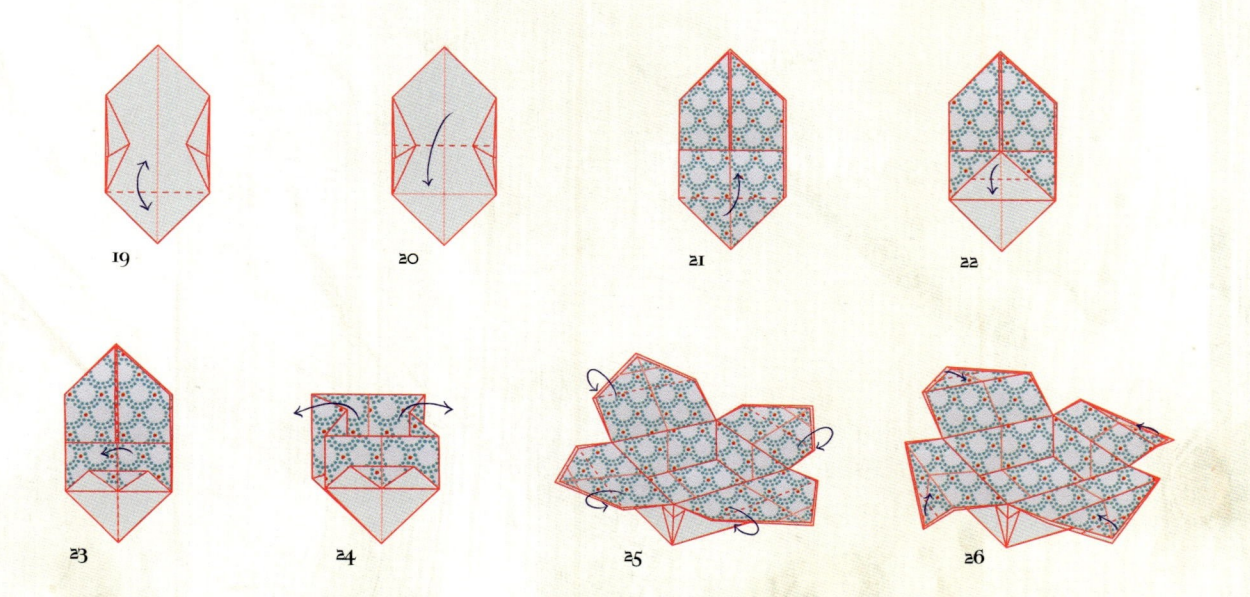

19   20   21   22

23   24   25   26

assembly

Make the folding for the box following the instructions.
  Measure a square 22 x 22cm (8¾ x 8¾in) on to a sheet of greaseproof paper. Check the corners using a set square. Make another box out of this paper. Slip this new box inside the first so that it can be filled with food. Put your biscuits inside and close the box, following the shape that the folds naturally fall into at the top.

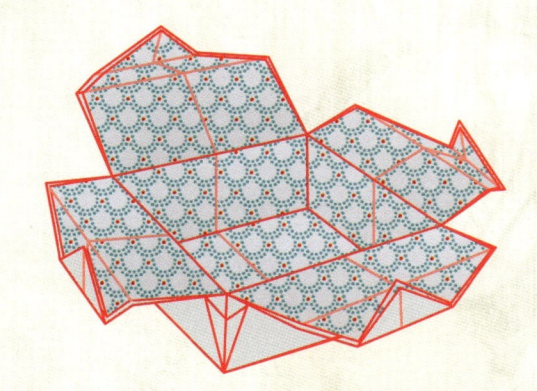

japanese dolls

let's have a tea party!

japanese dolls

MATERIALS FOR ONE DOLL

1 sheet of patterned Japanese paper 30 x 7cm (11¾ x 2¾in) ◆ 1 sheet of matching Japanese paper 3.8 x 9cm (1½ x 3½in) ◆ 1 rectangle of Japanese paper 1.5 x 3.8cm (½ x 1½in) ◆ 1 scrap of patterned origami paper ◆ 1 scrap of white paper ◆ 1 scrap of black paper ◆ tracing paper ◆ black paint ◆ scrap of origami paper

EQUIPMENT

1 pencil ◆ 1 craft knife ◆ 1 cutting mat ◆ 1 ruler ◆ 1 paper folder ◆ 1 tube of adhesive ◆ 1 paintbrush ◆ 1 pink coloured pencil ◆ 1 pair of scissors

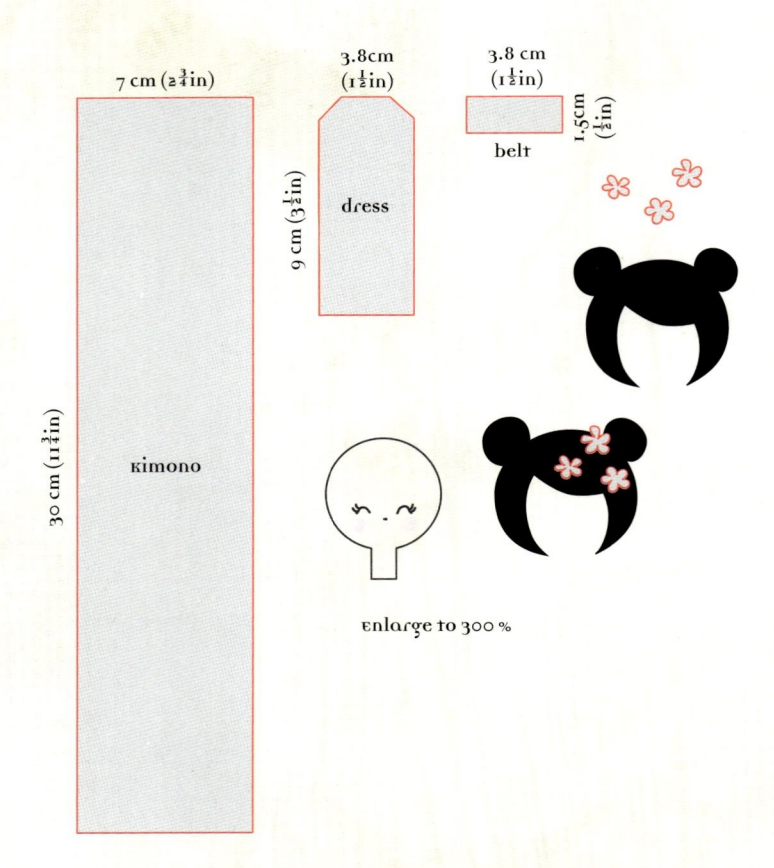

7 cm (2¾in)

3.8cm (1½in)

3.8 cm (1½in)

1.5cm (½in)

belt

dress

9 cm (3½in)

30 cm (11¾in)

kimono

enlarge to 300 %

152

for children

difficulty ♦♦

folding

1. Fold along the dotted line to make a collar.
2. Turn the folding over.
3. Mark the centre of the bottom of the folding using a pencil. Fold along the dotted lines.
4. Fold along the dotted line.

1   2   3   4

153

japanese dolls (cont.)

5. Turn the folding over.
6. Fold over to the front along the dotted line.
7. Flip the fold over and fold the first sheet along the dotted line.
8. Flatten the folding. Slide the fold made beneath the collar.
9. Fold along the dotted line to make a fold in the kimono.
10. Repeat steps 7 to 9 with the left side.
11. Fold the shoulders over to the rear, without folding the collar.
12. Cut out the dress and the belt. Glue the belt to the dress. Slide into the kimono from the bottom and secure in place with a spot of adhesive. See the next section for assembling the head.

for children

assembly

Trace the face from the design provided on to a sheet of white paper. Paint the eyes with a paintbrush and black paint. Leave to dry. Add colour to the cheeks with a pink coloured pencil.

Trace the hair template on to the reverse of a sheet of black paper. Cut out with the scissors. Glue the hair to the face.

Trace the design for the three flowers to the reverse of a scrap of origami paper. Cut out with a pair of scissors. Glue on to the hair.

Slide the neck into the collar. Secure in place with a spot of adhesive.

9

10

11

12

let's have a tea party!

MATERIALS

1 sheet of patterned origami paper 20 x 20cm (7¾ x 7¾in) for the tea pot ◆ 1 sheet of matching origami paper 5 x 5cm (2 x 2in) for the lid ◆ 4 squares of patterned origami paper 8 x 8cm (3¼ x 3¼in) for the cups ◆ 2 scraps of patterned Japanese paper for the spout of the tea pot ◆ 1 scrap of white paper ◆ 1 leather cord 10cm (4in)

EQUIPMENT

1 craft knife ◆ 1 cutting mat ◆ 1 ruler ◆ 1 paper folder ◆ 1 tube of adhesive ◆ 1 pair of scissor

folding the cup

1. Fold a patterned square of paper 8 x 8cm (3¼ x 3¼in) in half along the diagonal of the square.
2. Fold the right-hand point to the left along the dotted line, so that the right-hand point reaches the opposite edge.
3. Fold over the left-hand point along the dotted line.
4. Fold over the first top sheet towards the bottom along the dotted line.
5. Cut the point of the first sheet along the blue line.
6. Turn the folding over.
7. Fold over the sheet towards the bottom following the dotted line.
8. Cut along the blue line.
9. Open the cup to give it its shape. Press underneath the cup to flatten out the base. Fold the points towards the centre. Stand on a flat surface so that the cup stays upright.

folding the tea pot

For the body of the tea pot, take a patterned square of paper 20 x 20cm (7¾ x 7¾in) and follow the instruction for folding a cube on page 22–23.

for children

difficulty 🔴🔴

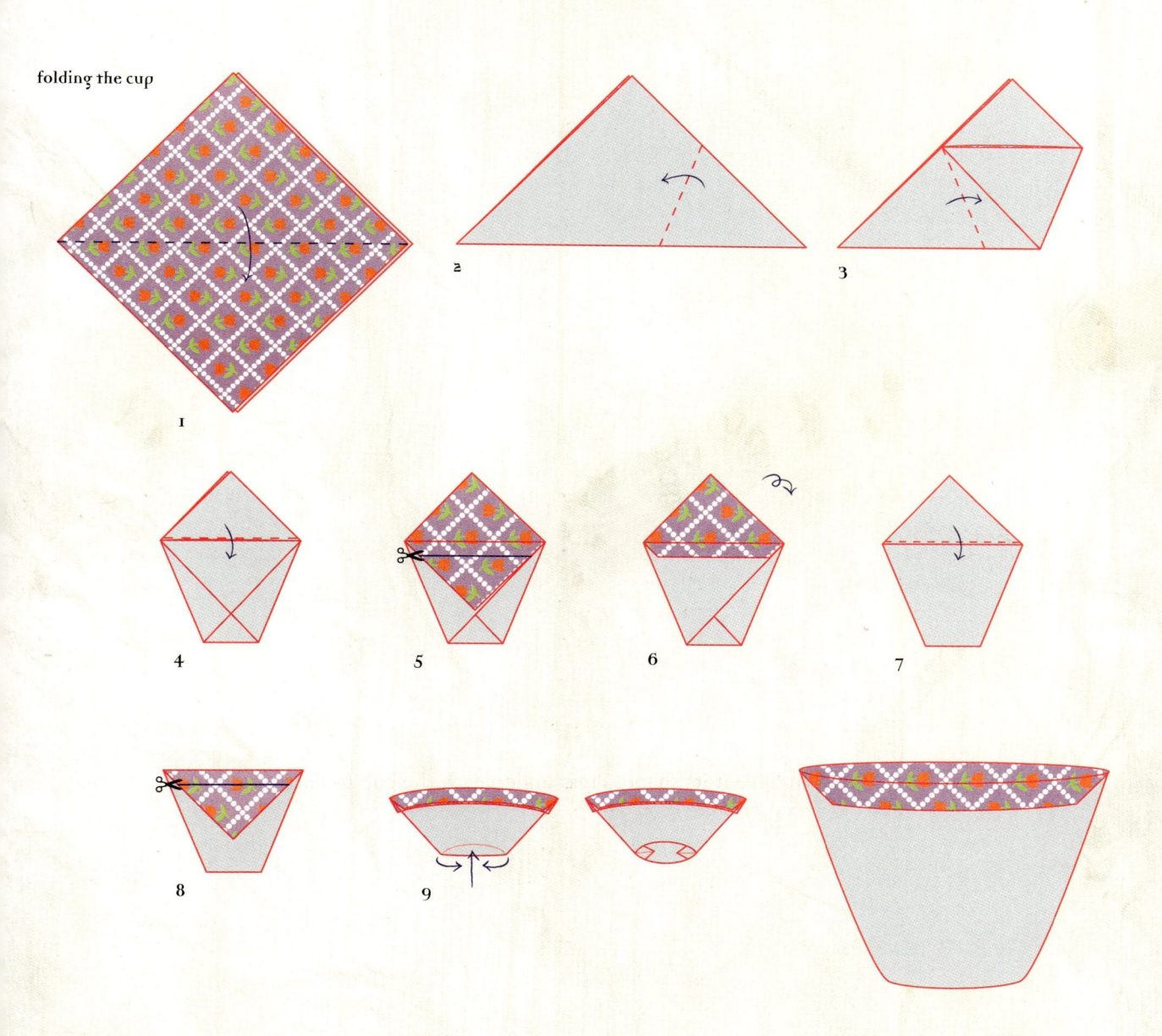

folding the cup

1
2
3
4
5
6
7
8
9

let's have a tea party! (cont.)

folding the lid

1. Take a patterned square 5 x 5cm (2 x 2in). Fold along the centre lines. Unfold. Fold in half downwards along the horizontal.
2. Fold along the dotted lines.
3. Open the folding up completely and re-fold in half along the vertical central line.
4. Fold along the dotted lines.
5. Open the folding without unfolding the centre line folds. If necessary, make the folds again to form a cone.
6. Turn the folding over.
7. Fold to the rear along the dotted lines.
8. Fold the points to the rear.

assembly

Trace the spout of the tea pot from the template provided. Transfer to a sheet of white paper. Cut out with a pair of scissors.

Cover the two sides with the same paper as for the body of the tea pot without glueing the base of the spout. Smooth with your hand and leave to dry. Cut out.

Open the base of the spout as in the diagram. Spread adhesive on these inside edges and glue inside one of the vertical folds of the tea pot.

Glue the lid to the top of the tea pot. Slide one end of the leather cord into a fold on the side of the cube. Secure in place with a spot of glue. Do the same with the other side of the cord attaching to the pot. Leave to dry.

for children

folding the lid:

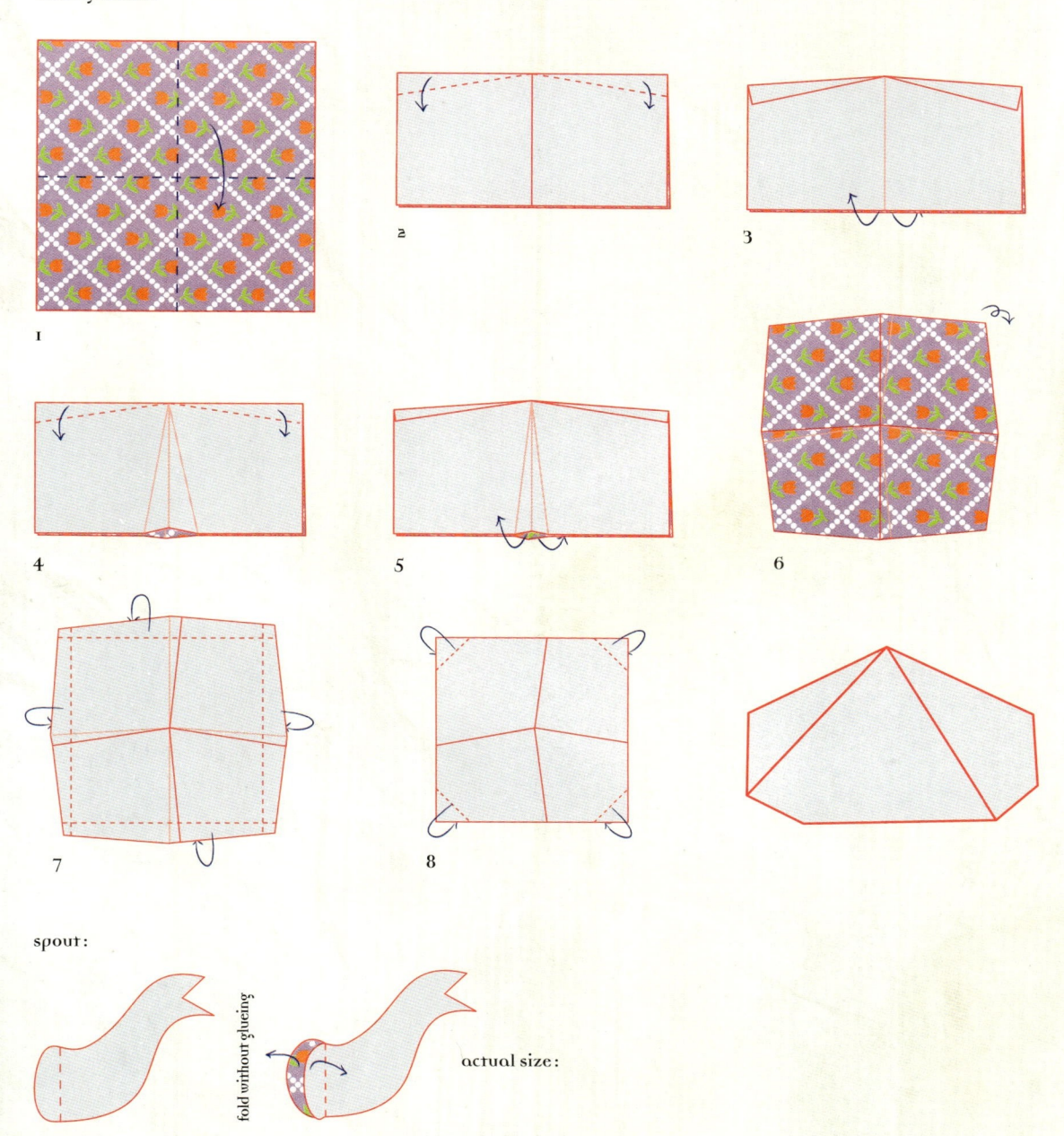

1
2
3
4
5
6
7
8

spout:

fold without glueing

actual size:

159